Enter the
COMPLEXITY
LAB

Enter the

COMPLEXITY
LAB

William Roetzheim

Copyright © 1994 by Sams Publishing

SAMS
PUBLISHING

A Division of
Prentice Hall Computer Publishing
201 West 103rd Street,
Indianapolis, Indiana 46290

FIRST EDITION

International Standard Book Number: 0-672-30395-7

Library of Congress Catalog Card Number: 93-85112

97 96 95 94   4 3 2 1

Interpretation of the printing code: the rightmost double-
digit number is the year of the book's printing; the
rightmost single-digit, the number of the book's printing.
For example, a printing code of 94-1 shows that the first
printing of the book occurred in 1994.

*Composed in Palatino and MCPdigital by Prentice Hall
Computer Publishing*

Printed in the United States of America

Trademarks

PUBLISHER
Richard K. Swadley

ASSOCIATE PUBLISHER
Jordan Gold

ACQUISITIONS MANAGER
Stacy Hiquet

MANAGING EDITOR
Cindy Morrow

DEVELOPMENT EDITOR
Rosemarie Graham

PRODUCTION EDITOR
Sandy Doell

COPY EDITOR
David Bradford

EDITORIAL AND GRAPHICS COORDINATOR
Bill Whitmer

EDITORIAL ASSISTANTS
Sharon Cox
Lynette Quinn

TECHNICAL REVIEWER
Susan Sulzbach

MARKETING MANAGER
Greg Wiegand

COVER DESIGNER
Jean Bisesi

DIRECTOR OF PRODUCTION AND MANUFACTURING
Jeff Valler

IMPRINT MANAGER
Kelli Widdifield

MANUFACTURING COORDINATOR
Barry Pruett

BOOK DESIGNER
Michele Laseau

PRODUCTION ANALYST
Mary Beth Wakefield

PROOFREADING/INDEXING COORDINATOR
Joelynn Gifford

GRAPHICS IMAGE SPECIALISTS
Tim Montgomery
Susan VandeWalle

INDEXER
Craig A. Small

PRODUCTION
Gary Adair, Katy Bodenmiller,
Brad Chinn, Kim Cofer, Meshell Dinn,
Mark Enochs, Diana Bigham-Griffin,
Stephanie Gregory, Jenny Kucera,
Beth Rago, Marc Shecter, Greg Simsic,
Carol Stamile

Dedication

A rock, providing an island of stability
against the backdrop of a churning sea of uncertainty;

A candle, emitting emotional warmth and light
that holds back the enveloping darkness;

A haven, nurturing and supporting the children
that provide immortality to a transient existence;

A companion, sharing adventures and quiet respites
with equal joy and comfortable satisfaction.

To my wife, Marianne.

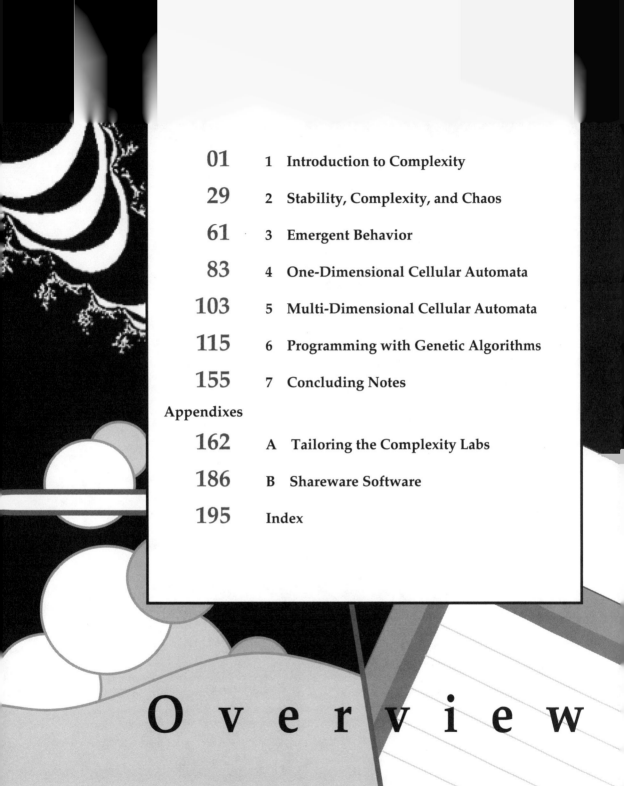

Overview

Contents

3   Emergent Behavior   61

4   One-Dimensional Cellular Automata   83

7   Concluding NOTES   155

Appendixes

A   Tailoring the Complexity Labs   161

Acknowledgments

I would like to thank Susan Sulzbach for her help with the technical accuracy of this book. I would also like to thank the following individuals who helped in the production of this book: Stacy Hiquet, Rosemarie Graham, Sandy Doell, Wayne Blankenbeckler, and David Bradford.

About the Author

William H. Roetzheim is an internationally recognized authority on software engineering (project management, software documentation, cost estimating, risk analysis), C and C++. He lectures frequently, writes numerous articles, and has written many widely recognized books, including *Uncharted Windows Programming* from Sams Publishing. Three of his books have been featured selections of the month by McGraw-Hill Library of Computer Science Book Club.

His work is noted for its clarity and readability, even when the topic is extremely complicated and technical. He is Senior Associate with the consulting firm of Booz-Allen & Hamilton, the largest management and technology consulting company in the world with over 4,500 employees in offices on five continents.

Introduction

Who Should Read This Book

If you are not a computer programmer but are simply interested in complexity, have no fear. You can learn about and experiment with all aspects of complexity by reading this book and running the Complexity Lab application program. Although code fragments are included in the body of the book, I attempted to keep the listings and their explanations in the "For Programmers Only" sections to enable nonprogrammers to skip those sections.

If you are interested in the source code, note that all of the code examples in this book use C++, and I start off assuming that you are familiar with this language. If you need some help learning C++, pick up any of the dozens of excellent introductory books on the topic. I also assume that you are already familiar with Windows programming using C++ and Borland's Object Windows Library (OWL). If you're new to either topic, you may want to read my book *Programming Windows With Borland C++* or the more advanced (and difficult) *Uncharted Windows Programming*. Finally, I assume that you are fluent in MS-DOS and Windows. Basically, to understand the source code included in this book you should be completely comfortable writing, compiling, and debugging a Microsoft Windows program in C++.

Computer Requirements

To run the sample programs found on the Complexity Lab disk included with this book, you will need at least an 80386 computer, 4M of memory, a mouse, an 80M hard disk, and a VGA card and monitor. To successfully modify and recompile the source code, also found on the disk, you will need a larger hard disk (100M or more). Because many of the applications of complexity theory are computationally intense, faster central processing units (CPUs) and more memory are certainly in order if you plan to work with the sample applications at length.

The programs in this book were tested using Borland C++ version 3.1 and its accompanying Application Framework. The Application Framework provides tools to build and edit program resources (the Resource Workshop) and the Object Windows Library (OWL) to simplify Windows development using C++. If you are using the Turbo C++ for Windows compiler, all of the programs should run without problems. Code that is not OWL specific should work properly with the Microsoft C++ compiler, although I have not personally tested code using Microsoft C++.

In addition to a version of the Borland compiler, you must have a copy of Microsoft Windows version 3.1 or later. Examples in this book were tested using version 3.1.

Conventions Used in This Book

The following typographic conventions are used in this book:

- Code lines, commands, statements, variables, and any text you see on the screen appear in a `computer` typeface.
- Command output and anything that you type appears in a **`bold computer`** typeface.
- Placeholders in syntax descriptions appear in an *`italic computer`* typeface. Replace the placeholder with the actual filename, parameter, or whatever element it represents.
- *Italics* highlight technical terms when they first appear in the text, and are sometimes used to emphasize important points.

Each chapter begins with a glossary of important terms introduced in that chapter. This glossary is designed to help you be alert for the important points you will encounter in that chapter.

The Complexity Lab icon is used throughout this book to denote references to material contained on the Complexity Lab disk.

What's on the Disk

The disk that accompanies this book contains the executable version of the Complexity Lab application (COMPLEX.EXE). This program enables you to run all of the sample programs described in this book. In addition, programmers should note that the disk contains files to be used with the examples throughout the book. The disk will save you hours of typing and debugging.

Format for This Book

This is a hands-on, see-it-for-yourself kind of book. I begin each chapter by describing a key concept of complexity. Each chapter includes a computer model that demonstrates the concept visually. These models are run from a Microsoft Windows program called COMPLEX, and I refer to the samples as exercises in the Complexity Lab.

Chapter 1, "Introduction to Complexity," includes a working definition of complexity and an overview of the contents of the disk.

Chapter 2, "Stability, Chaos, and Complexity," discusses stability, complexity, and chaos. I expand on my definition of stability and chaos, then demonstrate each using a Complexity Laboratory program called Attractors. I then discuss chaos in more depth, demonstrating some interesting characteristics of chaos using a Complexity Laboratory program called Fractals.

Chapter 3, "Emergent Behavior," focuses on emergent behavior as it pertains to things such as colony insects, birds, and cell development. An implementation of a classic computer program in this area, Boids, is used in the Complexity Lab to provide a startling example of emergent behavior.

Chapter 4, "One-Dimensional Cellular Automata," focuses on a simple-to-program (yet surprisingly beautiful and interesting) computer modeling technique called one-dimensional cellular automata. An interactive program called Tapestry is used in the Complexity Lab to visually demonstrate the behavior of a system as it makes the transition from stable to chaotic to complex behavior.

Chapter 5, "Multi-Dimensional Cellular Automata," extends the concept of one-dimensional cellular automata to multiple dimensions and describes how this modeling technique can be applicable to a wide range of problems. Another classic from the world of complexity theory, Life, is used in the Complexity Lab.

One fascinating area where complexity both predicts and models complicated, emergent behavior is in the field of genetic programming, introduced in Chapter 6, "Programming with Genetic Algorithms." In fact, these two fields are so tightly intertwined that no discussion of complexity would be complete without illustrations from this well-known offshoot. The Complexity Lab program demonstrates genetically learned maze-running behavior in the Mice in a Maze experiment.

Chapter 7 presents some closing observations.

Because the basic computer code for the Complexity Laboratory application itself is not central to understanding complexity theories, I have chosen to include this code in the "For Programmers Only" sections. In Appendix A, "Tailoring the Complexity Labs," you learn how to build upon the basic tools provided on the disk to create your own, unique programs.

Appendix B, "Shareware Software," is a discussion of the shareware programs included with the Complexity Lab. If you find these programs useful and want to continue to experiment with them, I encourage you to support the shareware concept by sending the program's author(s) the requested fees (which are quite nominal).

After reading this book, you may wish to correspond with me about the subject matter. I invite you to do so by U.S. mail at 13518 Jamul Drive, Jamul, CA 91935 or via CompuServe at 71542, 1717. I am also available for paid consulting support through Booz-Allen and Hamilton, Inc. (619/223-5681).

Getting Started on Your Adventure

You do not have to be a scientist to *Enter the Complexity Lab*, or even an expert in computer programming. Without further ado, open the door and enter the world of Complexity.

Chapter

1

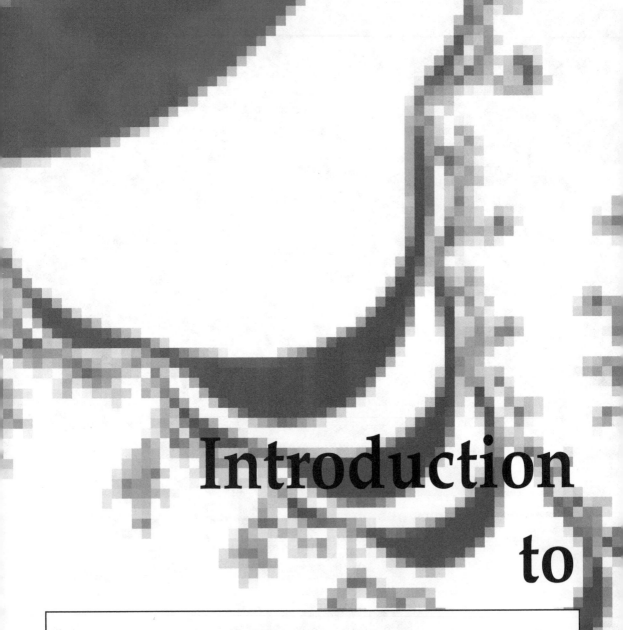

Introduction to

to

COMPLEXITY

COMPLEXITY

The state of being complex or intricate, changing.

CHAOS

Acting in a seemingly random fashion with no patterns, no memory, and no emergent behavior.

STABILITY

Something that isn't changing. In a complex system stability is death.

The world is not a simple place. Your body consists of trillions of cells, all interacting to keep you alive and healthy. Your brain consists of billions of neurons, all interacting to allow you to think and remember. The stock market consists of millions of people like you, all interacting to create a market with behavior that virtually every analyst describes as if it were a living entity.

Traditional science focuses on understanding the individual pieces of a problem. How does a cell work? How does a neuron work? How does an individual investor behave? Tremendous strides have been made in answering these questions. The next logical step was to take knowledge about the individual components and use that knowledge to understand the behavior of groups of components. That didn't work. No matter how thoroughly scientists analyze each of the types of cells in your body, they get no closer to understanding how these cells interact. For example, what makes one cell decide to be a liver cell, while a nearby cell decides to become part of a blood vessel? No matter how thoroughly scientists analyze each of the neurons in your brain, they get no closer to understanding how human thought works. For example, how is memory stored? No matter how thoroughly economists analyze individual investor behavior, they get no closer to understanding the behavior of the stock market. For example, what caused the market to suddenly and unexpectedly fall 500 points in October of 1987?

The answers to these and myriad other real-world questions may be found in a new field of science called complexity theory. This book explores many aspects of this fascinating field, explaining concepts through the use of examples and experiments rather than mathematics and theory. I hope that you find the ideas fun and invigorating and that you gain insight into the underlying concepts. Those of you with a more mathematical or theoretical interest will then be ready to delve into the mathematically intensive papers and books that are available.

I also need to caution you at this early stage in the book. The science of complexity is very new, and because of this the theories are evolving rapidly. If complexity theory were software, I would characterize it as just entering alpha (early) testing! Because of this, take what I say with a grain of salt. Question everything. Some avenues you explore in this book may be branches of complexity theory that look promising now but turn into dead ends. Other branches may be waiting to be discovered. Don't limit your mind's creative abilities by taking everything I say at face value. *You* may be the person destined to make the next major discovery and perhaps win the Nobel prize.

A Working Definition of Complexity

Complexity theory applies to all branches of study that deal with interacting things. Chapter 7, "Concluding Notes," provides some examples from fields as diverse as medicine, economics, and biology. The study of complexity was not possible prior to the widespread availability of computers. Computers are integral to complexity theory because the interacting systems can be modeled and observed on a computer but can't be defined and studied using traditional experiments or mathematics. Because complexity is a relatively new branch of science, much of the work is still theoretical, and early experiments tend to be better at helping us understand the way things are than at performing some specific task.

Complexity is so new that authors of existing books haven't really tried to define it. If they worry about it at all, they use analogies and examples to convey the general concept. Webster's defines *complexity* as "…anything complex or intricate…" and defines *complex* as "…a group of related ideas, activities, things, etc. that form, or are viewed as forming, a single whole." Although my definition of complexity as it applies to complexity science is similar, it is somewhat more precise. I define *complexity science* as

> The study of emergent behavior exhibited by interacting components operating at the threshold of stability and chaos.

To understand this definition, and hence the science of complexity, you need to understand each of the three parts of this definition.

The Study of Emergent Behavior…

Seemingly complicated behavior can actually be quite predictable. An automaton at Walt Disney World moves, speaks, and generally behaves in an amazingly lifelike way, yet each of its movements and gestures was preordained at the time its programs were written. It responds in a preprogrammed way to the environment and has no ability to adapt to change. If the individual who programmed it watched for hours on end, he or she would never observe anything that was surprising or unexpected.

Complex systems exhibit complicated behavior that is not predictable. A programmer who develops a complex model on the computer frequently observes behavior that is surprising or unexpected. The behavior was not programmed in from the beginning, but it emerged as the program operated. I term this unexpected, nonprogrammed behavior *emergent behavior*. Chapter 3, "Emergent Behavior," presents a clear example of a seemingly simple program that exhibits complicated, emergent behavior. Other programs described in the remaining chapters of this book go on to provide additional examples of the prevalence of emergent behavior in complex systems.

...Exhibited by Interacting Components...

The behavior of individual things is best studied using traditional science, and this behavior is seldom surprising. An individual cell behaves in a predictable fashion, as does an individual neuron and, to a large extent, an individual investor. It is only when these individual components interact with each other, and influence each other through these interactions, that the system as a whole begins to exhibit complex, emergent behavior. By definition, the science of complexity is the study of the behavior of the *system* and the interaction of its individual components (not the behavior of the individual components). You will discover that all of the example programs in this book consist of interacting components.

...Operating at the Threshold of Stability and Chaos.

The interaction among components can be structured to force the system into a static or repeating state. Perhaps the interacting pieces all eventually turn red. Perhaps they cycle between red and blue. As you slightly perturb the system (change it), it eventually returns to the same stable state. As you perturb the system in a major way, it eventually returns to the same or another stable state. Stability is interesting, but it is not complex. For living systems, stability also is not adaptable to change. In complex systems that exhibit lifelike, emergent behavior, stability is death.

The interaction among components also can be so intense and varying that the individual components exhibit quasi-random behavior. The system as a whole consists of myriad components interacting in a seemingly random fashion with no patterns, no memory, and no emergent behavior. These systems are said to be chaotic. In living systems, chaos prevents the organism from retaining traits that are good. In complex systems, chaos is often pretty but largely useless.

A single interacting system is stable with certain parameter values and chaotic with others. These conditions of the system are often called phases, as in *chaotic phase*. As the parameter values are adjusted from those that result in stable behavior to those that result in chaotic behavior, a transition in system behavior occurs. At the exact values where this phase transition occurs, the system begins to exhibit the emergent behavior that I character-ize as *complex*. It is chaotic enough to adapt and seek out new behaviors, but stable enough to hold onto those that work.

All living systems operate continuously in this narrow phase transition region between stability and chaos, this region of complexity. They don't exist here because they choose to, but because the interacting forces operat-ing on them force them to this region. Stable interactions are forced to become more chaotic. Chaotic interactions are forced to become more stable. The system finds itself pressed between two conflicting demands, driven inexorably to balance within the narrow, but optimal, region between stability and chaos.

Later in this book I provide more specific descriptions of stability and chaos and demonstrate the behavior of a visual system (a one-dimensional cellular automaton) as it changes from stability through complexity to chaos.

Running the Complexity Lab

During installation, a program group called "Enter the Complexity Lab" was created and the Complexity Lab icon along with icons for three shareware programs were installed into this program group. To run the Complexity Lab, double-click the Complexity icon. The screen shown in Figure 1.1 is displayed.

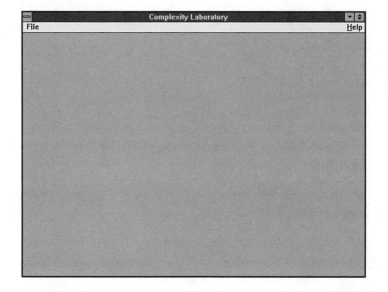

Figure 1.1.
Complexity Lab main screen.

Most chapters in this book make use of one or more experiments within the Complexity Lab. To run an experiment, select File from the main menu (Figure 1.2), then select the experiment to run. I have designed the Complexity Lab so that you can simultaneously run and monitor multiple experiments or multiple versions of one experiment. Because the Complexity Lab takes advantage of the multitasking capabilities of Windows, you can easily run your experiments in the background while you work on other projects. In addition, you can obtain online help for any application by selecting Help, Index. See Figure 1.3.

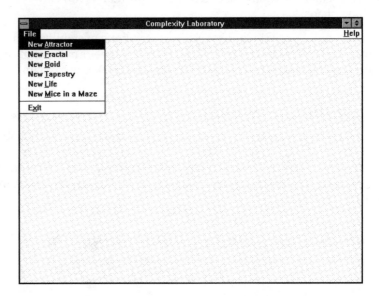

Figure 1.2.
Complexity Lab
File menu.

Enter the COMPLEXITY LAB

For Programmers Only

As previously mentioned, the Complexity Lab was implemented in C++ using the Borland C++ compiler and the Borland Object Windows Library. It was designed using object-oriented design techniques, both to enhance your ability to modify the code through encapsulation of capabilities in discrete objects, and to enable you to easily reuse and extend the classes in your own applications related to this topic.

The approach I used to implement the Complexity Lab was a typical example of the strength of Windows development using object-oriented programming languages. I implemented the Complexity Lab's main window and the multiple document interface (MDI) child window for each of the labs (Attractor, Fractal, and so on). These child windows did nothing but display a text string that said, `This is the XYZ Window paint function.` where *XYZ* was replaced with the name of the specific MDI window. I also implemented a setup dialog box for each lab that had no field other than the Speed field, which is present for all labs. During this process I implemented all of the resources in a generic format. For example, the icons and bitmaps were black backgrounds with the text "Boid", "Fract", and so on. Finally, I implemented the complete set of online help text with the text simply saying "*XYZ* help text." with *XYZ* replaced with the name of the lab. At this point I had a fully functional application, with stubs for all code that still had to be developed. I then began, one lab at a time, to replace the stubs with functional code. I simultaneously replaced the external resources (bitmaps, icons, help file text, and so on) with the appropriate specific data. A reviewer (or end user, in your applications) can watch the application evolve and review components while other components are still being built. This approach to rapid prototyping, in which user-oriented functional capability is added piece by piece, is called *threaded prototyping*.

I store only one class in each file. The files are named based on the class names (or as close as I can get for longer class names) and consist of a file with an .H prefix that contains the class header and a file with a .CPP prefix that contains the implementation of the class member functions.

Class Relationships and Overview

Table 1.1 summarizes the function of each class in the Complexity Lab. This table is called an *object dictionary* and serves roughly the same purpose as a data dictionary in a database application.

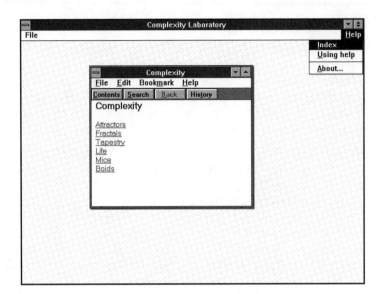

Figure 1.3.
Complexity Lab online help.

Table 1.1. Complexity Lab Object Dictionary

Object	Description
TStreamable	Base class for all objects that are streamable. Streamable objects can be written to disk and later read back in from disk.
WStr	Class that provides string handling capabilities.
TWindowsObject	Base class for many windows objects that have characteristics of a window.
TWindow	A Microsoft Windows window.
TMDIFrame	The Windows multiple document interface allows one application to work on several things at once, each in its own window. The TMDIFrame encapsulates the main window frame. The Complexity Lab is an MDI application.
WComplexFrame	This is the Complexity Lab version of the TMDIFrame.

Enter the COMPLEXITY LAB

Object	Description
WDragWindow	The WDragWindow class gives a window support for the user marking an area of the screen by using the mouse to drag a rectangle around the area. Each Complexity Lab application window inherits from the WDragWindow class.
WComplexBase	This class provides generic capabilities exhibited by each of the specific Complexity Lab window classes. One example of functionality it provides to all derived classes is support for the windows timer mechanism to support updates to the window.
WAttractorWindow	This is the MDI window for the Attractor lab.
WBoidWindow	This is the MDI window for the Boid lab.
WFractalWindow	This is the MDI window for the Fractal lab.
WLifeWindow	This is the MDI window for the Life lab.
WMiceWindow	This is the MDI window for the Mice in a Maze lab.
WTapestryWindow	This is the MDI window for the Tapestry lab.
TControl	Class that provides generic capabilities for controls such as those in dialog boxes.
TButton	Class that handles push buttons such as the OK push button in a dialog box.
TCheckBox	Class that handles check boxes.
TBCheckBox	Class that handles the Borland style check boxes.
TRadioButton	Class that handles radio buttons.
TGroupBox	Class that handles group controls.
TStatic	Class that handles static text controls.
TEdit	Class that handles edit fields.
TDialog	Generic handler for dialog boxes.
WAttractorDialog	The dialog handler for the Attractor lab setup dialog box.

continues

Table 1.1. continued

Object	Description
WBoidDialog	The dialog handler for the Boid lab setup dialog box.
WFractalDialog	The dialog handler for the Fractal lab setup dialog box.
WLifeDialog	The dialog handler for the Life lab setup dialog box.
WMiceDialog	The dialog handler for the Mice in a Maze lab setup dialog box.
WTapestryDialog	The dialog handler for the Tapestry lab setup dialog box.
TScroller	Class that provides scrolling capability for a window.
Object	Abstract class that is the starting point for many of Borland's classes.
TModule	Class that encapsulates generic capabilities of a running application.
TApplication	Class that encapsulates a running application.
WComplex	The Complexity Lab running application.
TMessage	An encapsulated windows message.
WBit	This class allows data to be stored in a bit array and easily manipulated on a bit-by-bit basis. It is useful for storing a large number of Boolean values.
WBoid	This class encapsulates many characteristics of an individual boid in the Boid lab.
WBox	Class that encapsulates a rectangular region with built-in knowledge about how to draw itself and erase itself. This class is used by the WDragWindow class.
WMice	This class encapsulates many characteristics of an individual mouse in the Mice in a Maze lab.
WMouseRule	This class encapsulates an individual genetic rule in the Mice in a Maze lab.

Enter the COMPLEXITY LAB

Object	Description
AttractorTransfer	Transfer buffer for the Attractor dialog class.
BoidTransfer	Transfer buffer for the Boid dialog class.
FractalTransfer	Transfer buffer for the Fractal dialog class.
LifeTransfer	Transfer buffer for the Life dialog class.
MiceTransfer	Transfer buffer for the Mice in a Maze dialog class.
TapestryTransfer	Transfer buffer for the Tapestry dialog class.

Figure 1.4 illustrates the complete complexity laboratory class inheritance hierarchy. In object-oriented design, an *inheritance hierarchy* is used to show the kind of relationships between the various classes. For example, in this figure you can see that a WMiceWindow is a kind of WComplexBase, which is a kind of WDragWindow, which is a kind of TWindow, which is a kind of TWindowsObject, which is a kind of TStreamable. Classes that are shown by themselves (that is, at the bottom of the figure) are stand-alone classes that do not inherit characteristics from any other class. The classes that begin with a T are provided by Borland with the compiler. The classes that begin with a W were developed for this application. The classes that include the word Transfer (for example, TapestryTransfer and FractalTransfer) are structs that are used as transfer buffers to communicate with the setup dialog box for each individual laboratory. These objects are defined in the header files for the dialog classes.

Figure 1.5 is the Complexity Lab's class creation diagram. This diagram shows the classes that create other classes in the application.

Class Design

The Complexity Lab program uses seven generic classes that are applicable to all of the laboratories. These are WComplex, WComplexFrame, WDragWindow, WComplexBase, WStr, WBit, and WBox. WComplex and WComplexFrame encapsulate the Complexity Lab application and the MDI frame, so these top level classes are specific to this application. WStr, WDragWindow, WBit, and WBox are four classes I use in many of my applications to provide generally useful capabilities. WComplexBase provides capabilities that are specific to the Complexity Lab application but are used by all of the individual laboratories. I'll now discuss each of the seven generic classes briefly.

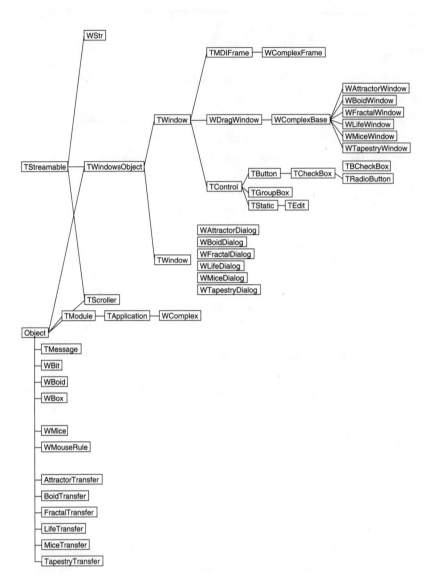

Figure 1.4.
*The Complexity
Lab class
hierarchy.*

Enter the COMPLEXITY LAB

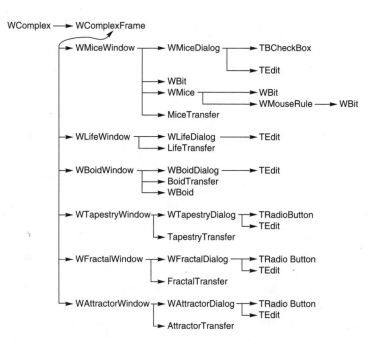

Figure 1.5.
The Complexity Lab class creation diagram.

WComplex

Figure 1.6 shows the class design for the WComplex class. The figure is a class design specification using a variant of the Multi-View Object Oriented Design (MOOD) method, which is based in turn on the Coad-Yourdon OOD method. The class is shown as a rectangle with the class name appearing at the top. Member functions that put data into the class, or cause the class to perform some action, are shown on the left side with arrows leading into the class rectangle. These are called *input functions*. Member functions that primarily extract data from the class or are actions initiated by the class itself are shown on the right side with arrows leading out from the rectangle. These are called *output functions*. The function prototypes for all input and output functions are shown below the class rectangle. The WComplex class encapsulates the running application and is descended from Borland's TApplication, which does most of the work. Its only function is to initialize the main complexity MDI frame (WComplexFrame) and start the application running.

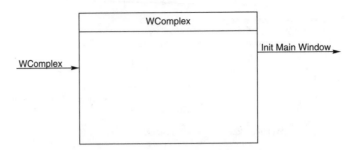

Figure 1.6.
WComplex class
design.

```
WComplex (LPSTR szName,HINSTANCE hInstance,
          HINSTANCE hPrevInstance,LPSTR lpCmdLine,
          int nCmdShow);
virtual void InitMainWindow ();
```

WComplexFrame

Figure 1.7 shows the class design for the WComplexFrame class. The class data members are shown within the class rectangle in the diagram. The Boolean flag Valid and member function IsValid() are static so that they will be available even if the WComplexFrame class is invalid (for example, never created). The WComplexFrame class is the MDI frame window in which the various Complexity Lab child windows will reside. It is responsible for creating the appropriate child windows in response to the selected menu choice and ensuring that the displayed menu properly matches the active child window. (Each child window has its own menu that must be displayed at the top of the frame window.) It also handles the arrangement of child windows on the screen, supporting functions such as Cascade and Tile. Table 1.2 summarizes the purpose of each of the WComplexFrame member functions.

Table 1.2. WComplexFrame Member Functions

Member Function	Purpose
WComplexFrame	Constructor.
~WComplexFrame	Destructor.
IsValid	Tests to see if the MDI frame window is valid. Used by the child windows.
GetClassName	Returns "WComplexFrame".
GetWindowClass	Returns the window class. Used to set the custom icon for the window.

Enter the COMPLEXITY LAB

Member Function	Purpose
SetMenu	Selects the appropriate menu based on the active child window.
ChildBirth	Used when a new child window is created.
ChildDeath	Used when a child window is destroyed. The MDI frame must be prepared to display its default menu when no more child windows exist.
Attractor	Creates the Attractor Lab child window.
Fractal	Creates the Fractal Lab child window.
Boid	Creates the Boid Lab child window.
Tapestry	Creates the Tapestry Lab child window.
Life	Creates the Life Lab child window.
Mice	Creates the Mice in a Maze child window.
Exit	Closes the MDI frame window and all of its children.
About	Displays the generic About Complexity Lab box.
HelpIndex	Displays the online help index.
HelpHelp	Displays help on how to use the online help system.

WDragWindow

Figure 1.8 shows the class design for the WDragWindow class. As you can see from the figure, WDragWindow contains another class, WBox. The relationship between WBox and WDragWindow is called a *class-containment relationship*. WDragWindow is an ancestor of all of Complexity Lab child windows. Table 1.3 summarizes the purpose of each of the WDragWindow member functions. This class provides automatic support for allowing the user to specify a rectangular region on the screen using the mouse. The window that wishes to use this support simply needs to intercept the message indicating that the left mouse button has been released and take whatever action is desired for the specified rectangle. In the Complexity Lab this capability is used to specify a region on the fractal map for zooming, and to add rectangular barriers for the Boid and Mice in a Maze programs. Once again, this is a class for which I have found numerous uses over the years.

Figure 1.7.
WComplexFrame
class design.

```
WComplexFrame (WStr Title);
~WComplexFrame ();

static BOOL IsValid();
LPSTR GetClassName ();
void GetWindowClass (WNDCLASS&);
void SetMenu (WStr Name, int ChildPos);
void ChildBirth ();
void ChildDeath ();

void Attractor (RTMessage)=
        [CM_FIRST+CM_Attractors];
void Fractal (RTMessage)=[CM_FIRST+CM_Fractals];
void Boid (RTMessage)=[CM_FIRST+CM_Boid];
void Tapestry (RTMessage)=[CM_FIRST+CM_Tapestry];
void Life (RTMessage)=[CM_FIRST+CM_Life];
void Mice (RTMessage)=[CM_FIRST+CM_Mice];
void Exit (RTMessage)=[CM_FIRST+CM_Exit];
void About (RTMessage)=[CM_FIRST+CM_About];
void HelpIndex ()(RTMessage)=[CM_FIRST+CM_HelpIndex];
void HelpHelp ()(RTMessage)=[CM_FIRST+CM_HelpHelp];
```

Table 1.3. `WDragWindow` Member Function Descriptions

Member Function	Description
WDragWindow	Constructor.
WMLButtonDown	Starts the drag operation.
WMMouseMove	Displays a dotted rectangle as the mouse is dragged.
WMLButtonUp	Erases the dotted rectangle and sets the rectangular coordinates in the WBox object, DragRect, based on the final outlined area.

Enter the COMPLEXITY LAB

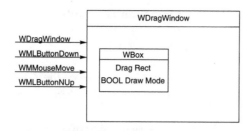

Figure 1.8.
WDragWindow
class design.

```
WDragWindow (PTWindowsObject,LPSTR,PTModule);

    virtual void WMLButtonDown (RTMessage)
        =[WM_FIRST+WM_LBUTTONDOWN];
    virtual void WMMouseMove (RTMessage)
        =[WM_FIRST+WM_MOUSEMOVE];
    virtual void WMLButtonUp (RTMessage)
        =[WM_FIRST+WM_LBUTTONUP];
```

WComplexBase

Figure 1.9 shows the class design for the **WComplexBase** class. This class provides general capabilities that are useful for all of the individual complexity labs. Table 1.4 describes each of the member functions in the class.

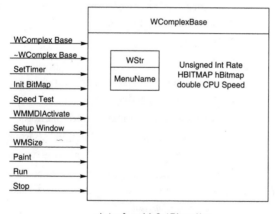

Figure 1.9.
WComplexBase
class design.

```
virtual void SetTimer();
void InitBitmap();
double SpeedTest();

WComplexBase(PTWindowsObject Frame,LPSTR Name);
virtual~WComplexBase();

void WMMDIActivate (RTMessage);
void SetupWindow();
void WMSize (RTMessage);
void Paint (HDC,PAINTSTRUCT&);

void Run (RTMessage)=[CM_FIRST+CM_Run];
void Stop ()=[CM_FIRST+CM_STOP];
```

CHAPTER ONE **Introduction to Complexity**

Table 1.4. WComplexBase Member Function Descriptions

Member Function	Description
SetTimer	Sets a Windows timer based on the Rate. This timer then drives the Update function in each of the individual labs.
InitBitmap	The WComplexBase function stores the screen contents in a bitmap. This allows the screen to be repainted (that is, after icons are minimized) without repeating all of the calculations. This function initializes the bitmapped screen image.
SpeedTest	This function initializes the CPUSpeed variable, which is used for loop counters in the Update function of many labs. The loop counters allow the application to properly balance lab calculations with other Windows requirements (that is, processing mouse movements). A CPUSpeed of 1.0 is the equivalent of the computer I did the testing on. A CPUSpeed of .5 would be roughly one-half as fast as my computer, so the loop counters would also be cut in half.
WComplexBase	Constructor.
~WComplexBase	Destructor.
WMMDIActivate	Whenever a lab is activated, this function ensures that the proper menu is displayed.
SetupWindow	Performs windows initialization functions.
WMSize	Processed to allow the window bitmap image to be properly resized when the window is resized.
Paint	Standard Windows paint function. The default behavior for the complexity labs is to display the stored screen image bitmap.
Run	Handles the Run menu choice in each complexity lab by starting the windows timer.
Stop	Handles the Stop menu choice in each complexity lab by stopping the windows timer.

Enter the COMPLEXITY LAB

WStr

Figure 1.10 shows the class design for the WStr class. This class provides general-purpose string-handling capabilities. It is a mainstay of my programming toolbox. Table 1.5 shows the purpose of each member function. It was necessary to make some of the overloaded operators friend functions rather than member functions to allow you to do functions such as

```
WStr    Temp1 = "Hello" + "World";
```

Because the first argument to the operator + is a string literal and not a WStr object, the compiler would not know to look for a WStr member function in order to handle this case. Friend functions override the way the compiler handles operator + acting on a char*, which solves the problem quite nicely.

Table 1.5. WStr Member Function Descriptions

Member Function	Description
streamableName	Returns "WStr". Used for streamable classes.
WStr	Constructors.
~WStr	Destructors.
Length	Returns length of the string.
Find	Finds an embedded string.
Slice	Returns a segment from a string.
write	Writes string to disk.
read	Reads string from disk.
DeleteAll	Resets the string to null.
build	Creates a default string prior to reading one from disk.
ToInt	Converts a string to an integer.
ToLong	Converts a string to a long.
ToDouble	Converts a string to a double.
operator char *	Converts a string to a char *.
operator +	Concatenates two strings.

continues

CHAPTER ONE   **Introduction to Complexity**

Table 1.5. continued

Member Function	Description
operator -	Extracts one string from another.
operator ^	Exclusive or two strings (useful for encryption).
operator =	Assigns one string to another.
operator +=	Concatenates and assigns.
operator -=	Finds, removes, and assigns.
operator ^=	Exclusive or and assign.
operator <	Test less than.
operator >	Test greater than.
operator <=	Test less than or equal.
operator >=	Test greater than or equal.
operator ==	Test for equality.
operator !=	Test for not equal.
ToString	Family of functions to convert numeric values into WStr objects.

WBit

Figure 1.11 shows the WBit class design. This class supports an array of Boolean values, storing one value in each bit of a character array rather than requiring a complete byte for each Boolean value. It has an overhead of 10 bytes (12 bytes for compilers that use 4-byte integers); it is not very efficient for bit arrays less than 12 bits in length, but it saves quite a bit of space for larger arrays. If you need to use it for smaller arrays and space is at a premium, you could modify it to have only 6 bytes of overhead by limiting the number of bits that can be stored to 64K (use an unsigned short rather than a long for Size and calculate the value for Bytes rather than storing it). The WBit class does not replace the more efficient approach of using a bit type in a struct for hardware type bit manipulation, but it is much better when working with larger bit arrays and bit arrays that change in size. In the Complexity Lab, I used it extensively in the Mice in a Maze lab when implementing the genetic algorithms. Table 1.6 summarizes the member functions of the WBit class.

Enter the COMPLEXITY LAB

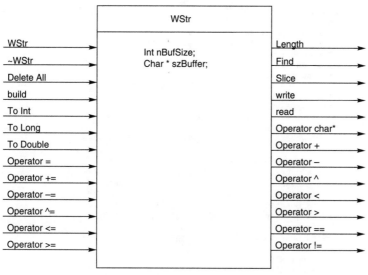

WStr	
WStr	Int nBufSize;
~WStr	Char * szBuffer;

WStr → | | → Length
~WStr → | | → Find
Delete All → | | → Slice
build → | | → write
To Int → | | → read
To Long → | | → Operator char*
To Double → | | → Operator +
Operator = → | | → Operator –
Operator += → | | → Operator ^
Operator –= → | | → Operator <
Operator ^= → | | → Operator >
Operator <= → | | → Operator ==
Operator >= → | | → Operator !=

Figure 1.10.
WStr *class design.*

```
virtual const Pchar streamableName ()const;
        WStr (StreamableInit);

        WStr ();                    //Default constructor
        WStr (char*szText);//Create from C string
        WStr (int nSize);//Create setting buffer size
        WStr (WStr& sString);  //Create from existing String

        ~WStr ();

        int Length ();             //Get length
        int Find (WStr& sString, int nStart=0);
        int Find (char* szString, int nStart=0);
        char Slice (int nCharacter);   //Get character
        WStr Slice (int nStart, int nStop); //Get Slice

        virtual void write (Ropstream);
        virtual Pvoid read (Ripstream);
        void DeleteAll ();   //helper function
        static PTStreamable build ();

        int ToInt();       //Convert string to int
        long ToLong();     //Convert string to long
        double ToDouble(); //Convert string to double

        operator char*(); //Convert string to C style
```

Figure 1.10.
continued

```
WStr operator+(WStr&String);
WStr operator+(char*szString);
friend Wstr operator+
        (char*szString1, WStr&sString2);
WStr operator-(WStr&sString);
WStr operator-(char*szString);
friend Wstr operator-
        (char *szString1, WStr&sString2);

WStr operator^(Wstr&sString2);

WStr operator^(char *szString2);
friend WStr operator^ (char*szString1, Wstr&sString2);

WStr& Operator=(Wstr&sString);     //Assignment
WStr& Operator=(char*szString);    //Assignment
WStr& Operator+=(WStr&sString);    //Concatenate
WStr& Operator+=(char*szString);   //Concatenate
WStr& Operator-=(WStr&sString);    //Find & Remove
WStr& Operator-=(char*szString);   //Find & Remove
WStr& Operator^=(WStr&sString);    //EOR
WStr& Operator^=(char*szString);   //EOR

BOOL operator<(WStr&sString);
Bool operator<(char*szString);
friend BOOL operator<(char*szString1, WStr&sString2);
BOOL operator>(WStr&sString);
Bool operator>(char*szString);
friend BOOL operator>(char*szString1, WStr&sString2);
BOOL operator<=(WStr&sString);
Bool operator<=(char*szString);
friend BOOL operator<=(char*szString1, WStr&sString2);
BOOL operator>=(WStr&sString);
Bool operator>=(char*szString);
friend BOOL operator>=(char*szString1, WStr&sString2);

BOOL operator==(WStr&sString);
Bool operator==(char*szString);
friend BOOL operator==(char*szString1, WStr&sString2);
BOOL operator!=(WStr&sString);
Bool operator!=(char*szString);
friend BOOL operator!=(char*szString1, WStr&sString2);

WStr ToString (int nValue, WStr sFormat = "%d");
WStr ToString (int nValue, char*szString);

WStr ToString (long 1Value, WStr sFormat = "%d");
WStr ToString (long 1Value, char*szString);

WStr ToString (double dValue, WStr sFormat = "%f");
WStr ToString (double dValue, char*szString);
```

Table 1.6. WBit Member Functions

Member Function	Description
WBit	Constructor.
~WBit	Destructor.

Enter the COMPLEXITY LAB

Member Function	Description
Error	Internal function to display an error message if you try to write or read past the allocated size of the array.
SetMask	Internal helper function that puts a 1 in the appropriate bit position of a byte.
ResetAll	Resets all values to defaults.
ClearAll	Clears all bits in the bit array.
SetAll	Sets all bits in the bit array.
Set	Sets a specific bit to 1.
ClassName	Returns "WBit".
GetSize	Returns the size of the bit array.
Test	Returns 0 if a specific bit is on, 1 otherwise.
Clear	Clears a specific bit.
Toggle	Toggles the specified bit.
Random	Sets the specified bit to a random value (1 or 0).
operator =	Sets one bit array equal to another. The bit arrays do not need to be the same size.

WBox

Figure 1.12 summarizes the class design for the WBox class. This class is used by WDragWindow to draw and erase the dotted rectangle on the screen. The member functions are described in Table 1.7.

Table 1.7. WBox Class Member Functions

Member Function	Description
WBox	Constructor.
DeleteAll	Resets all values to defaults.
Frame	Draws the rectangle using a dotted exclusive OR pen. The exclusive OR pen is used to allow the rectangle to be erased by drawing it again at the same location.

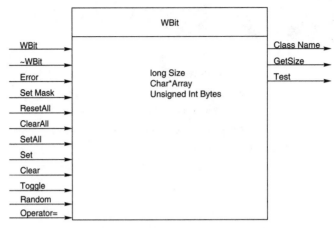

Figure 1.11.
WBit class design.

```
void Error ();
unsigned char SetMask (int Bit);

WBit ();
WBit (long MaxElements);
virtual~WBit ();

virtual void ResetAll(void);
virtual WStr ClassName ();

long GetSize ();
void ClearAll ();
void SetAll ();
BOOL Test (long Element);
void Set (long Element);
void Clear (long Element);
void Toggle (long Element);
void Random ();

WBit & operator= (RWBit);
WBit & operator= (PWBit);
```

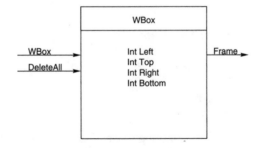

Figure 1.12.
WBox class description.

```
WBox(void); //initializer
WBox(int,int,int,int);
void Frame(HDC);
void DeleteAll();
```

Enter the COMPLEXITY LAB

Complexity Lab Resources

Table 1.8 summarizes the purpose of each of the resources included in the Complexity Lab's resource file, COMPLEX.RC.

Table 1.8. Resources in COMPLEX.RC

Type	Identifier	Description
Bitmap	MiceBitmap	Bitmap for Mice in a Maze splash panel on About dialog box.
Bitmap	ComplexBitmap	Bitmap for Complexity Lab splash panel on About dialog box.
Bitmap	AttractorBitmap	Bitmap for Attractor Lab splash panel on About dialog box.
Bitmap	FractalBitmap	Bitmap for Fractal Lab splash panel on About dialog box.
Bitmap	BoidsBitmap	Bitmap for Boids Lab splash panel on About dialog box.
Bitmap	TapestryBitmap	Bitmap for Tapestry Lab splash panel on About dialog box.
Bitmap	LifeBitmap	Bitmap for Life Lab splash panel on About dialog box.
Menu	AttractorMenu	Menu for Attractor Lab MDI window.
Menu	BoidsMenu	Menu for Boids Lab MDI window.
Menu	ComplexMenu	Default menu for Complexity Lab.
Menu	FractalMenu	Menu for Fractal Lab MDI window.
Menu	LifeMenu	Menu for Life Lab MDI window.
Menu	MiceMenu	Menu for Mice in a Maze MDI window.
Menu	TapestryMenu	Menu for Tapestry MDI window.
Dialog	AttractorAbout	About box for Attractor Lab.
Dialog	AttractorDialog	Setup dialog box for Attractor Lab.
Dialog	BoidsAbout	About box for Boids Lab.
Dialog	BoidsDialog	Setup dialog box for Boids Lab.
Dialog	ComplexAbout	About box for Complexity Lab.

continues

Table 1.8. continued

Type	Identifier	Description
Dialog	FractalAbout	About box for Fractal Lab.
Dialog	FractalDialog	Setup dialog box for Fractal Lab.
Dialog	LifeAbout	About box for Life Lab.
Dialog	LifeDialog	Setup dialog box for Life Lab.
Dialog	MiceAbout	About box for Mice in a Maze Lab.
Dialog	MiceDialog	Setup dialog box for Mice in a Maze Lab.
Dialog	TapestryAbout	About box for Tapestry Lab.
Dialog	TapestryDialog	Setup dialog box for Tapestry Lab.
Icon	AttractorIcon	Icon displayed when you minimize the Attractor Lab.
Icon	BoidsIcon	Icon displayed when you minimize the Boids Lab.
Icon	ComplexIcon	Icon displayed when you minimize the Complexity Lab.
Icon	FractalIcon	Icon displayed when you minimize the Fractal Lab.
Icon	LifeIcon	Icon displayed when you minimize the Life Lab.
Icon	MiceIcon	Icon displayed when you minimize the Mice Lab.
Icon	TapestryIcon	Icon displayed when you minimize the Tapestry Lab.

Enter the COMPLEXITY LAB

Chapter

2

Stability,
Chaos,
and

COMPLEXITY

LINEAR BEHAVIOR

Behavior that can be described by equations with an order of magnitude of one.

NONLINEAR BEHAVIOR

Behavior that can only be described by equations with an order greater than one. Most systems in the real world exhibit nonlinear behavior and therefore can only be modeled by nonlinear equations.

COMPLEX NUMBERS

Numbers with both a real and an imaginary component.

IMAGINARY COMPONENT

In complex numbers, you can think of the real portion as representing the amplitude of the number, while the imaginary part represents the *phase*.

In Chapter 1, "Introduction to Complexity," I defined complexity as "the study of emergent behavior exhibited by interacting components operating at the threshold of stability and chaos." In this chapter I'll take a more in-depth look at the concept of stability and its antithesis, chaos. Using this understanding as a foundation, later chapters will take a high-level look at how the transition region between these two extremes provides a fertile ground for complicated system behavior.

This chapter includes two labs. *Attractors* enables you to visually explore various types of attractors, a fundamental concept of stability. *Fractals* enables you to explore the mathematically fascinating and visually breath-taking world of self-similarity often exhibited by chaos. I'll discuss both programs in more depth later in the chapter.

Stability, Chaos, and the Transition Between Them

The term *system* appears often in this book. By system I mean a collection of interacting components that can be studied in real life (for example, the stock market), simulated on a computer (for example, the spread of AIDS through the population), or modeled using mathematical equations (for example, the dispersion of a pollutant within a lake).

Stability

A *stable system* is one that exhibits repetitive behavior and tends to return to this behavior when artificially forced to a different behavior. For example, an ordinary pendulum is a stable system because it tends to hang straight down forever, and when forced to swing will eventually return to its stable position. The straight down position for a pendulum is called a *point attractor* because the pendulum is drawn to a specific point directly beneath the weight.

The real world contains many examples of stable systems. The planets in orbit around the sun are examples of stable behavior, where the attractor is an elliptical attractor (the orbit of a planet around the sun is an ellipse). A spinning gyroscope is stable, with an attractor forcing it to align itself to point toward the center of the earth. Many resource-based economic goods (farm products or minerals, for example) tend to exhibit stable behavior, in which the price and demand fluctuate in very predictable relationships with each other.

Many physical systems exhibit *linear behavior*. Linear behavior is behavior, exhibited by a system, that can be described by equations with an order of magnitude of one. For example, the equation

$$y = 2x$$

can be graphed as shown.

Enter the COMPLEXITY LAB

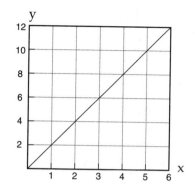

y is clearly dependent on x, but the dependency is linear because the dependent term on the right side of the equation has an order of magnitude of one. In other words, the dependent term is not raised to any power. Let's look at what happens if the equation were changed to

$$y = x^2$$

The order of magnitude for this equation is now 2, and the equation is no longer purely linear. A graph of this equation looks like this.

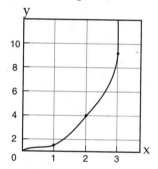

The Logistic Equation

It turns out that nonlinear equations are really quite common in the world. For example, a general equation called the logistic equation correctly models a wide range of situations in which a growing population competes for limited supplies. A good example might be fish in a lake that has a limited amount of food. When very few fish exist, they have plenty of food so they

CHAPTER TWO   **Stability, Chaos, and Complexity**

multiply like crazy. As the food becomes scarce, more fish die prior to reproducing and their numbers tend to level off. The logistic equation is

$$X_{n+1} = kX_n * (1 - X_n)$$

In this equation, n represents a time step (a generation of fish); X_{n+1} is the value of something for the current time step (the percent of fish, in this example); X_n is the value for the previous time step; and k is a problem-specific constant. X must be a number between 0 and 1, so the problem must be expressed accordingly—for example, by calling X the percent of total possible fish rather than the actual number of fish. This is a nonlinear equation with an order of magnitude of 2. To see this, multiply KX_n by both terms in the parenthesis to simplify the preceding equation to

$$X_{n+1} = kX_n - K(X_n)^2$$

The X_n^2 term determines the order of magnitude for the equation because it is the term with the highest power.

Recall that the constant k is a problem-specific constant. Let's look at what happens for various values of k. At k equal to 2, the system stabilizes at .5 for any starting value of X other than 0 and 1 (which stabilize immediately at 0). This is another example of a point attractor. For k equal to 2.5, the system stabilizes to about .6. For k equal to 3, the system oscillates between two points for a long time, eventually stabilizing. For k equal to 3.25 and X starting at .5, the system oscillates forever between .4952 and .8124. It has reached a stable pattern with two attractors. For k equal to 3.5, the system oscillates between 4 points. As K is increased from 3.5 to 4, the system oscillates between an ever-doubling number of points until, somewhere within this range, we say that the system has become chaotic.

Chaos

Chaos is the phenomena exhibited by some nonlinear systems in which interdependencies in the system (feedback) cause very small errors in the initial measurements (or in the precision of ongoing calculations) to be amplified to the point where the eventual result is unpredictable and widely varying.

You may be wondering why I call the behavior of the system for a high value of k (say k equal to 3.9) chaotic. Is it random? No, in fact, far from it. The formula for predicting future values of X is still just as simple. Given a value for X_n, I can easily plug it into the equation and determine the value for X_{n+1}. So I can accurately calculate the value for X at a given future step, right? Wrong! The problem is simple but profound. For chaotic systems, very minor variations in the initial parameters have an ever-increasing ripple effect on the final results until eventually, the final results are as dependent on the initial variation in measurement as on anything else. Increasingly accurate initial measurements enable you to make forecasts more and more iterations into the future, but you will always eventually be overwhelmed by that initial measurement error, no matter how small. Let's explore the implications of this in more detail.

 REAL WORLD

Actual. Nothing can be more chaotic than the battlefield, yet people writing war gaming software continued for years trying to force the models into easier-to-program and understand linear models. Over the past few years, researchers have been looking at ways to apply chaos theory to models of the battlefield, thus more accurately simulating the conditions a fighter or planner might experience in real life. The value of these improved simulations may go beyond better training. With the introduction of the chaotic component to the simulation, we may better model and anticipate some of the many illogical and devastating events that can be observed in the real-world history of people fighting people.

Nonlinear Dynamics and Chaos

One of the pioneers in chaos theory, Edward N. Lorenz, was working in the area of long-term weather forecasting, using computers to model the atmosphere. The underlying equations were manageable, although the computers took a considerable amount of time to complete the long series of calculations. One evening Lorenz needed to interrupt the computer to perform some other work. He copied down the equation's current value to use when he started the computer again. Rather than bothering to copy down all nine decimal places, he rounded the number off to four places. When he started the program where he left off, he entered this slightly changed number as a starting point and had the computer get back to work. After several iterations, the numbers diverged completely from those obtained before the introduction of the round-off error.

Was rounding off the number the problem? If he used the full precision of the computer, would the results be accurate? Lorenz did an experiment in which he changed the starting value by only a single place in the least significant digit represented by the machine's internal logic. Sure enough, after a long series of calculations the two results eventually diverged completely. Would machines with more precision eliminate the problem? No. No matter how accurately you make and represent that initial measurement, the characteristics of chaotic equations eventually overwhelm you and result in completely different results. Lorenz used the following example.

Suppose you are trying to predict the weather in Texas for the period six months from now. You make perfect initial measurements worldwide, but the flap of a single butterfly's wing in the Amazon is missed in your initial calculations. Because the entire planet's weather is interdependent in a nonlinear way, that butterfly wing has an impact on the weather in Texas— but isn't it so insignificant that we can ignore it? Unfortunately, no. The multiplying effect over the six-month prediction means that even that small measurement error will throw off your predictions completely, and the blue skies that you predict could be replaced by a tornado. This has become known as the Butterfly Effect.[1]

 REAL WORLD

Actual. One very valuable insight gained by chaos theory was simply that there are some things that we not only don't know, but can never know. For example, it is theoretically impossible to make accurate, detailed long-range weather predictions. Knowing this can save countless research dollars and hours in a fruitless pursuit for the equivalent of the alchemists lead to gold dream.

So, should we just give up? Of course not. First of all, systems that are linear *are* subject to accurate, long-range prediction. Successful flights to the moon are highly dependent on our ability to accurately predict the exact position of the moon at some future point. This is the reason that scientists often try to simplify or approximate a nonlinear system with a linear model. For stable nonlinear systems, you can make very accurate predictions about future behavior. For a value of k equal to 2 in the logistic equation covered in the previous section, we can safely predict an eventual value of .5 for any

1. Edward N. Lorenz, "Predictability: Does the Flap of a Butterfly Wing in Brazil Set Off a Tornado in Texas?," Address at the *Annual Meeting of the American Association for the Advancement of Science*, Washington, DC: December 29, 1979.

Enter the COMPLEXITY LAB

initial value of X. Clearly, initial measurement errors won't matter here. Even for chaotic, nonlinear systems, we can predict a short distance into the future. The distance to which we can safely look ahead is dependent on the accuracy of our initial measurements, the internal precision of the computer used to model the problem, and the degree of nonlinearity. All else being equal, equations that are close to linear can be predicted further into the future than equations with a higher order of nonlinearity.

REAL WORLD

Actual. Understanding and being able to model self-reinforcing systems that exhibit many traits of chaos have contributed greatly to our understanding of such diverse concepts as the driving force behind a hurricane or tornado and the turbulent flow of air across an airplane wing.

REAL WORLD

Actual. Many of the characteristics of chaotic equations make them ideal candidates for encryption algorithms. It is possible to start with a known initial value and determine the final value after a specified number of iterations (within limits), but it is virtually impossible to go from the final value back to the proper starting value without additional information. This trait is the key to good encryption algorithms. This is an active area of research.

Stable Attractors

Let's explore the world of stable attractors in nonlinear systems in more detail. The logistic equation gave us an example of a point attractor (k equal to 2) and a two-point oscillating attractor (k equal to 3.25), among others. To explore various types of attractors, we'll use the Attractor program in the Complexity Lab. If you're near your computer, run this application now by running the Complexity Lab, then selecting New Attractor from the File menu. Your screen should look like Figure 2.1. You may want to maximize both the Complexity Lab and the Attractor window to better see the results. You can do this by clicking the small arrow in the upper-right corner of each of these two windows.

Figure 2.1.
*Attractor
Window
running in the
Complexity Lab.*

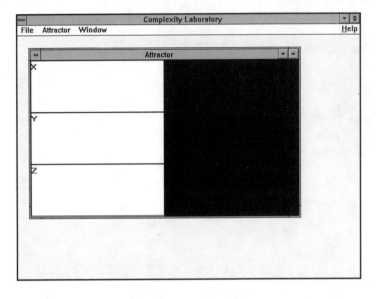

The Attractor window is divided into four subwindows. On the left, there is a plot for the X, Y, and Z parameters as they are calculated, and on the right, a window where the X and Y parameters are plotted in two dimensions. Using the Setup dialog box (accessed from the Attractor menu), you can change the various program parameters (see Figure 2.2). Table 2.1 describes the meaning of each field.

Table 2.1. Attractor Lab Setup dialog box fields and their default values

Field	Description	Default Value
Speed	Timer interrupt for program execution, in msec. 0 runs the maximum speed. 1000 would perform some calculations once every second. Use higher values when running in background.	0

Enter the COMPLEXITY LAB

Field	Description	Default Value
Delta T	Time step used when integrating the equations. Smaller values give more precision, larger values plot faster.	.04
Initial X	Initial X coordinate.	0
Initial Y	Initial Y coordinate	1
Initial Z	Initial Z coordinate	0
A Coefficient	First coefficient used in Lorenz and Julian equation (described below).	.2
B Coefficient	Second coefficient used in Lorenz and Julian equation.	.2
C Coefficient	Third coefficient used in Lorenz and Julian equation.	5.7
Points to Hide	The number of points to hide prior to outputting to the plot window on the right side of the Attractor main window. This is useful when you only want to plot values after the system is stable.	500
Points to Plot	The number of points to calculate and plot. Enter all numbers without commas.	10000
Type of Attractor	Julian or Lorenz	Julian

The Julian and Lorenz equations can be used to generate a wide variety of stable attractors, including point attractors, inward spirals toward a point at infinity, outward spirals toward infinity, circular orbits, and two types of *strange attractors*. Strange attractors are stable attractors that do not match a normal geometric shape (point, circle, ellipse, and so on). The two strange attractors available are the Julian and Lorenz attractors. To see each type of attractor, try starting with the values shown in Table 2.2, then experiment on your own. If you use parameters that overflow the math capabilities of the IBM PC, you get a warning dialog box. When this occurs, try using smaller values for X, Y, and Z or adjusting the Delta T value up or down.

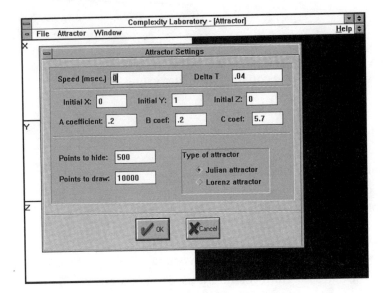

Figure 2.2.
Attractor Window setup dialog box.

Table 2.2. Attractor Lab settings for some types of attractors

Field	Point	Spiral Out	Spiral In	Circular	Lorenz	Julian
Speed	0	0	0	0	0	0
Delta T	.02	.04	.02	.04	.02	.04
Initial X	1	0	1	1	1	1
Initial Y	1	1	1	1	1	1
Initial Z	1	0	1	1	1	2
A Coefficient	0	0	20	.2	10	.2
B Coefficient	0	.2	20	.2	2.667	.2
C Coefficient	29	5.7	20	2	28	5.7
Points to Hide	0	0	0	0	500	500
Points to Plot	10000	10000	10000	10000	10000	10000
Basic Equation	Lorenz	Julian	Lorenz	Julian	Lorenz	Julian
See Figure	Figure 2.3	Figure 2.4	Figure 2.5	Figure 2.6	Figure 2.7	Figure 2.8
See Color Gallery					Yes	Yes

Enter the COMPLEXITY LAB

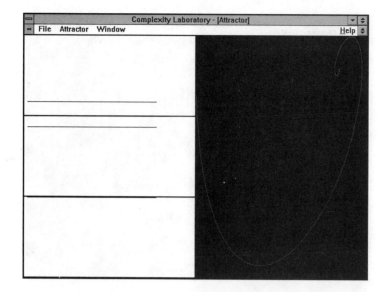

Figure 2.3.
Point attractor.

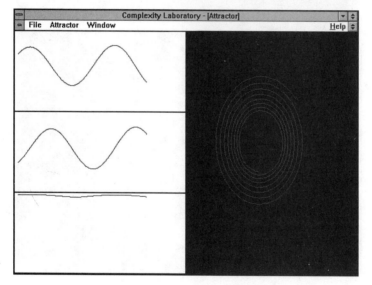

Figure 2.4.
Spiral out attractor.

CHAPTER TWO   **Stability, Chaos, and Complexity**

Figure 2.5.
Spiral in attractor.

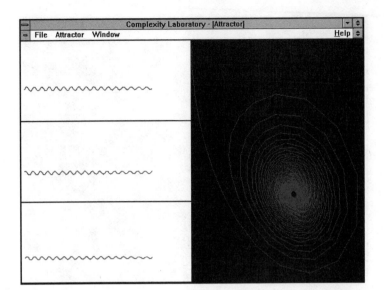

Figure 2.6.
Circular attractor.

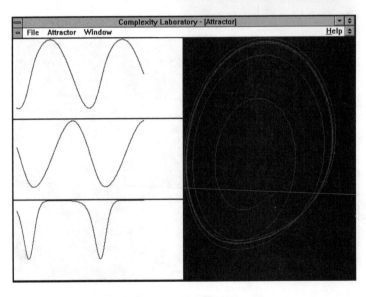

Enter the COMPLEXITY LAB

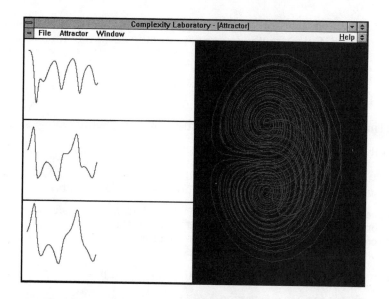

Figure 2.7.
Lorenz attractor (also see Color Gallery).

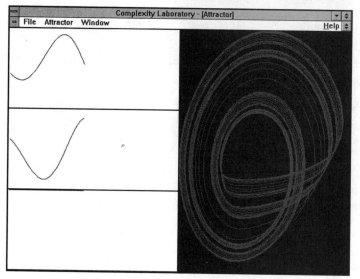

Figure 2.8.
Julian attractor (also see Color Gallery).

For both the Julian and Lorenz attractors, the function is evaluated using Euler's method. Euler's method approximates the new point for a function as

$$X_{n+1} = X_n + [\text{DeltaTime} * f(X_n)]$$

where

DeltaTime is the integration time increment from the Setup dialog, and;

f(X) is the function of interest (Lorenz or Julian)

Because I am performing the calculation for three dimensions (X, Y, and Z), I use the following code for my integration using Euler's method:

```
// approximate next value using Euler's method (first order method)
Function.X += (DeltaTime * EvaluatedFunction.X);
Function.Y += (DeltaTime * EvaluatedFunction.Y);
Function.Z += (DeltaTime * EvaluatedFunction.Z);
```

The actual function f(x) for the Julian attractor is as follows:

```
EvaluatedFunction.X = -Function.Y - Function.Z;
EvaluatedFunction.Y = Function.X + (CoefficientA * Function.Y);
➥EvaluatedFunction.Z = CoefficientB + (Function.X * Function.Z) -
(CoefficientC * Function.Z);
```

The variable Function is used to store the current value, and the variable Evaluated Function is used to store the new value.

The actual function f(x) for the Lorenz attractor is

```
EvaluatedFunction.X = (-CoefficientB * Function.X) + (Function.Z * Function.Y
➥EvaluatedFunction.Y = (CoefficientC * Function.Z) -
Function.Y - (Function.Z * Function.X);
EvaluatedFunction.Z =  CoefficientA * (Function.Y - Function.Z);
```

The code for the Attractor program is described in more detail in Appendix A, "Tailoring the Complexity Labs," along with the other programs in the Complexity Lab.

A Transition in Thinking

Prior to the 1980s, scientists went to incredible lengths to avoid nonlinear equations. During the early 1980s it became obvious that many of the messy, complicated systems in the world could be described only by nonlinear equations, and during the same time period computer simulations and new mathematical insights made nonlinear equations easier to work with. These equations have proven remarkably adept at describing a wide range of phenomena. For example, the theory of *solitons*, or self-sustained pulses of energy, describes the passage of water down a shallow canal and many subtle dynamics in quantum theory equally well. The Great Red Spot on Jupiter, a hurricane bigger than Earth, may be a soliton that has existed for at least 400 years.

 REAL WORLD

Potential. One of the all-time mysteries of life is how human thought works, and perhaps equally important, why it sometimes fails to work. It seems likely that thought does not consist of stored independent patterns such as might be found in a computer, but rather consists of interacting impulses that combine to create a stable pattern of interactions. Perhaps better understanding how this process works in computer modeled networks will help us understand it in humans, and perhaps watching how the patterns can be forced to chaos in the computer will help us understand the breakdown in the human thought process that is sometimes observed.

One interesting application of nonlinear dynamics is in the area of economics. Traditional economics is oriented toward economies in equilibrium, with deterministic dynamics. People are treated as identical and everything is assumed to be at, or striving toward, equilibrium. Traditional economics predicts decreasing returns, which can be summarized as "the more you have the less you get." The basic theory is that greater availability results in lower prices and decreased demand. Nonlinear dynamics predicts that some situations result in increasing returns, or "the more you have the more you get." In fact, many examples of increasing returns have been observed over the years. VHS dominates the video market today because early leads in consumer acceptance led to an ever-increasing market dominance. The more you have the more you get. The IBM PC class machine dominates the personal computer market not because the original IBM PC was the best hardware, or even the best value, but because its early lead led to a position of increasing market dominance. The more you have the more you get. Economic theory based on chaos and complexity has begun to use models from biology, based on structure, patterns, self-organization, and the life cycle, to model the economic process.

Let's look at some images of chaos close-up. We'll use the Complexity Lab program, *Fractals*, to explore various ways of looking at chaos.

Chaotic Patterns and Images

 REAL WORLD

Actual. One unanticipated benefit of chaos theory in general and the study of fractals in particular has been the degree of interest these phenomena have sparked in the artistic community. Many artists are now looking at computers as a potential medium for their art and expression, viewing the computer as a tool to create new images rather than simply a drawing tool. Looking at the images of chaos in this chapter, it is not hard to see why this is the case.

The nonlinear equations that we will be dealing with in Fractals use *complex numbers* for their calculations. Complex numbers are numbers with both a real and an imaginary component. The term *imaginary component* is actually a misnomer, because this part of the number is every bit as important as the real component. In complex numbers, you can think of the real portion as representing the amplitude of the number, while the imaginary part represents the *phase*. For wave phenomena, the phase represents whether the wave is at a peak, a valley, or somewhere in between. All of the examples in Fractals divide the Fractal window into a real plane along the X axis and an imaginary plane along the Y axis. This enables you to select any point in the window and tell its real component (the X value) and its imaginary component (the Y value).

For all of the numbers represented in our window's complex plane, we will look at the behavior of a simple nonlinear equation with an order of magnitude of two when given that number as a starting point.

$$Z = Z^2 + C$$

where

Z is a complex number; and

C is a complex number.

Enter the COMPLEXITY LAB

I iterate the equation, while watching the behavior of Z. If Z begins to go toward infinity, I stop and color the dot on the screen. The color I use is based on the number of iterations that were needed before it went out of bounds. If Z stays stable, I leave the screen location black.

Think about what you might expect to see in this situation. You might expect to see a fairly clear demarcation point where the numbers began to grow toward infinity. This point will often be one, with numbers below one going toward zero and numbers above one going toward infinity. Another possibility would be banding, perhaps with even numbers going to infinity and odd numbers remaining stable. Because we are dealing with the complex plane, it might be reasonable to have one or more quadrants in the plane go toward infinity with the remainder going toward zero.

Load the Fractal application and observe what really does happen. Figure 2.9 shows the available fields in the Fractal Lab's setup dialog box. Table 2.3 shows the meaning of each field. Start by using the default and selecting Run from the Fractal menu. A figure similar to Figure 2.10 should slowly appear. Be patient, because the calculations in this lab take quite a bit of time even on a fast PC. Using the default settings, the computer will need to do up to 470 million long-double floating-point multiples (among other operations) for each screen! The complex structure that finally emerges is not at all what we expected. In fact, this structure, called the Mandelbrot set, is so surprising and unique that it is named after the first scientist to discover it. The Fractal Lab includes the Mandelbrot set and another one called the Julian Set, both described in Table 2.3.

REAL WORLD

Actual. Some researchers are looking at exploiting the characteristics of chaotic equations to compress data. One demonstration of the power of this encryption approach is the simple fact that I can completely define any of the pictures of the Mandelbrot and Julian Sets simply by specifying the set, the horizontal and vertical ranges, the color map, and the number of iterations testing for divergence.

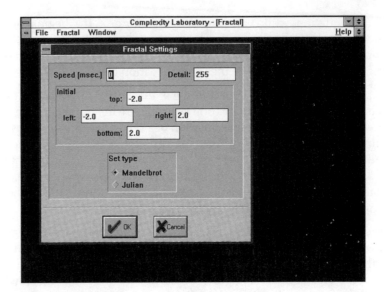

Figure 2.9.
Fractal Lab Setup Dialog Box.

Table 2.3. Available fields in the Fractal Lab's setup dialog box

Field	Description	Default Value
Speed	Timer interrupts for program execution, in msec. 0 runs the maximum speed. 1000 performs some calculations once every second. Use higher values when running in background.	0
Detail	The amount of detail to calculate/display for the plots. Lower numbers plot faster; higher numbers are more visually interesting and enable you to zoom in further. 16 is the minimum number (and results are borderline). 100 and up give good results. 255 gives excellent results and is recommended if you have the patience.	255

Enter the COMPLEXITY LAB

Field	Description	Default Value
Initial Left	Real axis start.	-2.0
Initial Top	Imaginary axis start.	-2.0
Initial Right	Real axis stop.	+2.0
Initial Bottom	Imaginary axis stop.	+2.0
Set Type	Used to select the Mandel-brot Set or Julian Set. The basic concept of each is similar, but the specific test for divergence is slightly different and the resulting visual images are significantly different.	Mandelbrot

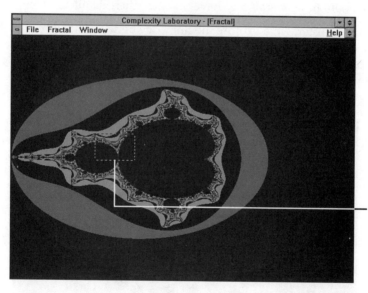

Figure 2.10.
The initial Mandelbrot Set (also see Color Gallery).

Area zoomed in on for Figure 2.11

Okay, so it's more complicated than expected when we use the default scale of -2 to +2 (real) and -2 to +2 (imaginary). As we zoom in, it should begin to simplify. After all, you wouldn't expect to see much difference in behavior for points scaled over, say, a .001 range. Figures 2.11 and 2.12 show the results of repeatedly zooming in on the Mandelbrot set (the dotted boxes in Figure 2.10 and 2.11 show the area being zoomed). In fact, you can zoom in on the Mandelbrot set to a degree limited only by the mathematical precision of your computer, and you will continue to see the same intricate structures. This is a visual portrait of chaos. Because it is a self-similar mathematical structure, it is also an extremely complex example of a fractal. It doesn't matter how narrow a region you chose—you will continue to find points that go to infinity (colored) and those that remain bounded (black). To experiment, start with a Mandelbrot set, then use the mouse to drag a rectangle over areas you would like to explore. (You do not need to select any menu choice to zoom; simply dragging the mouse is enough.)

By changing the test for divergence from the Mandelbrot Set to the Julian Set, we can significantly change the visual appearance of chaos. Figures 2.13, 2.14, and 2.15 show progressive zooms into the world of chaotic curls. It is significant to note the ever-repeating complexity of these spiral structures. You can zoom in on spirals and never exhaust their detail and complexity.

In the next chapter, we'll explore the fine edge between stability and chaos in more detail and examine why systems tend to be forced into this narrow transition region. I'll also present some fascinating theories about how complexity might explain such long-time mysteries as the emergence of life and the working of human memory.

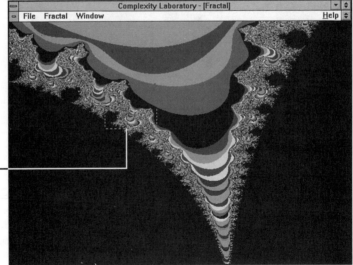

Figure 2.11.
Zoom-in on the Mandelbrot Set.

Area zoomed in ——
on for Figure 2.12

Enter the COMPLEXITY LAB

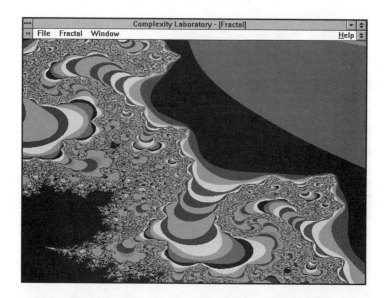

Figure 2.12.
*Mandelbrot Set
(also see Color
Gallery).*

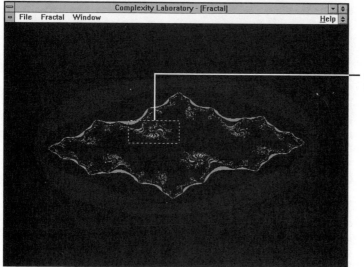

Area zoomed in
on for Figure 2.14

Figure 2.13.
*Chaotic curls
with default
settings.*

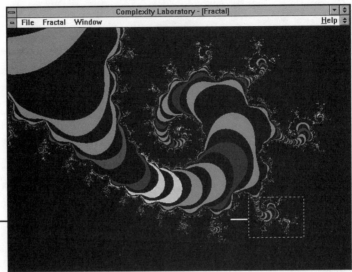

Figure 2.14.
Zoom in to chaotic curls.

Area zoomed in
on for Figure 2.15

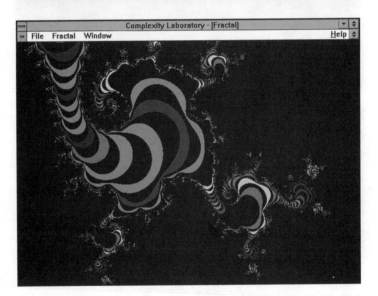

Figure 2.15.
A further zoom in on the chaotic curls (also see Color Gallery).

Enter the COMPLEXITY LAB

Suggested Further Reading

Peitgen, H., Jurgens, J., and Saupe, D., *Chaos and Fractals, New Frontiers of Science*, 1992, Springer-Verlag, New York. Expensive, but worth it. This book is the Bible of chaos. Over 1,000 pages long, with 686 illustrations (40 in color); very well-written and understandable. A must-have reference source.

Pickover, C., *Computers, Patterns, Chaos, and Beauty*, 1990, St. Martin's Press, New York. This is a fun book well worth the reasonable price. The author emphasizes the graphics and beauty of chaos rather than the underlying math and theories. Numerous applications of chaos theory to the real world are also explored in a fun, interesting way.

Hall, N., *Exploring Chaos: A Guide to the New Science of Disorder*, 1991, W.W. Norton & Company, New York. A midpriced overview of chaos with additional real-world examples of the application of chaos theory.

Pritchard, J., *The Chaos Cookbook*, 1992, Butterworth-Heinemann, Oxford, England. An expensive book with an emphasis on programming examples. Examples are presented in Pascal and Basic.

Cambel, A., *Applied Chaos Theory: A Paradigm for Complexity*, 1993, Academic Press, Inc., New York. An expensive book that presents chaos in a context of complexity theory. The approach is scholarly.

Arthur, B., "Positive Feedbacks in the Economy," *Scientific American*, February, 1990, pp. 92-99. A landmark paper in chaos and complexity as it applies to economic theory.

For Programmers Only

This Section describes the code and algorithms for the two complexity labs, Attractors and Fractals.

Attractors Lab

The Attractors Lab is implemented using two new classes. `WAttractorDialog` is a very simple class that handles the Attractor Lab Setup dialog box. A transfer buffer is used to communicate with the dialog box. This transfer buffer has the following structure:

```
// Transfer Buffer Used by WAttractorDialog
#define MAX_NUMERIC 11

struct AttractorTransfer
{
    char Rate [6];
    char InitialX [MAX_NUMERIC];
    char InitialY [MAX_NUMERIC];
    char InitialZ [MAX_NUMERIC];
    char ACoefficient [MAX_NUMERIC];
    char BCoefficient [MAX_NUMERIC];
    char CCoefficient [MAX_NUMERIC];
    char DeltaTime [MAX_NUMERIC];
    char PointsToHide [MAX_NUMERIC];
    char PointsToDraw [MAX_NUMERIC];
    WORD JulianAttractor;
    WORD LorenzAttractor;

    AttractorTransfer ()
    {
    strcpy (Rate, "0");
        strcpy (InitialX, "0");
        strcpy (InitialY, "1");
        strcpy (InitialZ, "0");
        strcpy (ACoefficient, ".2");
        strcpy (BCoefficient, ".2");
        strcpy (CCoefficient, "5.7");
        strcpy (DeltaTime, ".04");
        strcpy (PointsToHide, "500");
        strcpy (PointsToDraw, "10000");
        JulianAttractor = TRUE;
        LorenzAttractor = FALSE;
    };
};
```

Enter the COMPLEXITY LAB

One very useful programming technique is illustrated here. Because C++ considers structs to be objects in much the same way as classes, they can have constructors. The constructor in a struct is a useful way to initialize the values for each struct member. Putting the struct initiation code directly into the struct definition is the only exception I typically make to my general rule of not putting in-line code in a header file.

The WAttractorDialog class design is very simple.

WAttractorDialog Class

Figure 2.16 illustrates the class design for the WAttractorDialog class. Table 2.4 describes the single member function.

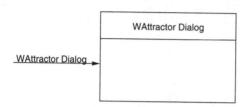

Figure 2.16.
*WAttractorDialog
class design.*

```
WAttractorDialog(PTWindowsObject Parent,
        struct AttractorTransfer*);
```

Table 2.4. WAttractorDialog Member Function Descriptions

Member Function	Description
WAttractorDialog	Constructor

WAttractorWindow Class

The WAttractorWindow class is a bit more interesting. The class design for this class is shown in Figure 2.17, and the member function descriptions are provided in Table 2.5.

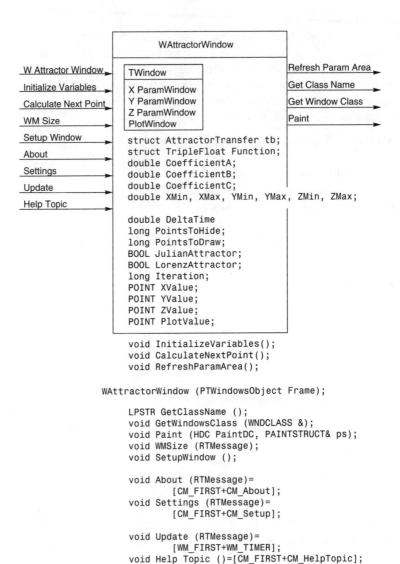

Figure 2.17.
WAttractorWindow
class design.

```
                    WAttractorWindow

                  TWindow                    Refresh Param Area

                  X ParamWindow              Get Class Name
                  Y ParamWindow              Get Window Class
                  Z ParamWindow
                  PlotWindow                 Paint

                  struct AttractorTransfer tb;
                  struct TripleFloat Function;
                  double CoefficientA;
                  double CoefficientB;
                  double CoefficientC;
                  double XMin, XMax, YMin, YMax, ZMin, ZMax;

                  double DeltaTime
                  long PointsToHide;
                  long PointsToDraw;
                  BOOL JulianAttractor;
                  BOOL LorenzAttractor;
                  long Iteration;
                  POINT XValue;
                  POINT YValue;
                  POINT ZValue;
                  POINT PlotValue;

                  void InitializeVariables();
                  void CalculateNextPoint();
                  void RefreshParamArea();

              WAttractorWindow (PTWindowsObject Frame);

                  LPSTR GetClassName ();
                  void GetWindowsClass (WNDCLASS &);
                  void Paint (HDC PaintDC, PAINTSTRUCT& ps);
                  void WMSize (RTMessage);
                  void SetupWindow ();

                  void About (RTMessage)=
                          [CM_FIRST+CM_About];
                  void Settings (RTMessage)=
                          [CM_FIRST+CM_Setup];

                  void Update (RTMessage)=
                          [WM_FIRST+WM_TIMER];
                  void Help Topic ()=[CM_FIRST+CM_HelpTopic];
```

Left-side labels:
W Attractor Window
Initialize Variables
Calculate Next Point
WM Size
Setup Window
About
Settings
Update
Help Topic

Table 2.5. WAttractorWindow Member Function Descriptions

Member Function	Description
WAttractorWindow	Constructor.
InitializeVariables	Private helper function to initialize all variables.

Enter the COMPLEXITY LAB

Member Function	Description
CalculateNextPoint	Private helper function to calculate the value for the next point.
WMSize	Processes the windows WM_SIZE message.
SetupWindow	Performs Windows initialization functions.
About	Displays the About dialog box for this lab.
Settings	Displays the Setup dialog box for this lab.
Update	Calculates and plots some points in response to a Windows timer message. The number of points plotted varies based on the speed of the CPU.
HelpTopic	Displays help specific to this lab.
RefreshParamArea	Clears the parameter area (where the X, Y, and Z values are plotted) when the plot line reaches the right boundary.
GetClassName	Returns "WAttractorWindow".
GetWindowClass	Returns the windows class. Used to set the icon to the proper value for this class.
Paint	Redraws the window.

Fractals Lab

Two classes, WFractalWindow and WFractalDialog, are used to implement the Fractals Lab. The transfer buffer used to communicate with the WFractalDialog class is as follows:

```
// Transfer Buffer Used by WFractalDialog
struct FractalTransfer
{
    char Rate [6];
    char Detail [6];
    char Left [11];
    char Top [11];
    char Right [11];
    char Bottom [11];
    WORD Mandelbrot;
    WORD ChaoticCurl;

    // structure initialization
```

```
FractalTransfer()
{
     strcpy (Rate, "0");
     strcpy (Detail, "255");
     strcpy (Left, "-2.0");
     strcpy (Top, "-2.0");
     strcpy (Right, "2.0");
     strcpy (Bottom, "2.0");
     Mandelbrot = TRUE;
     ChaoticCurl = FALSE;
  };
};
```

The character arrays correspond to the edit fields in the dialog box. The WORD values correspond to the radio buttons and can take on a value of TRUE or FALSE.

WFractalDialog

Figure 2.18 shows the design of the WFractalDialog class, and Table 2.6 describes the function of the single member function.

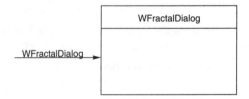

Figure 2.18.
WFractalDialog
class design.

```
WFractalDialog(PTWindowsObjectParent,
              struct FractalTransfer*);
```

Table 2.6. WFractalDialog Member Function Description

Member Function	Description
WFractalDialog	Constructor

WFractalWindow

Figure 2.19 illustrates the design of the WFractalWindow class, and Table 2.7 summarizes the purpose of each of the class member functions.

Enter the COMPLEXITY LAB

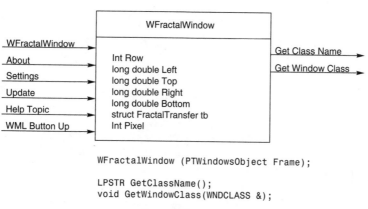

```
WFractalWindow (PTWindowsObject Frame);

LPSTR GetClassName();
void GetWindowClass(WNDCLASS &);

void About (RTMessage)=
        [CM_FIRST+CM_About];
void Settings (RTMessage)=
        [CM_FIRST+CM_Setup];
void Update (RTMessage)=
        [WM_FIRST+WM_TIMER];
void Help Topic ()=[CM_FIRST+CM_HelpTopic];
void WMLButtonUp (RTMessage)=
        [WM_FIRST+WM_LBUTTONUP];
```

Figure 2.19.
WFractalWindow
class design.

Table 2.7. `WFractalWindow` Member Function Descriptions

Member Function	Description
WFractalWindow	Constructor.
About	Displays the lab About dialog box.
Settings	Displays the lab Settings dialog box.
Update	Performs some calculations as a result of the Windows timer going off. The number of calculations performed is dependent on CPU speed.
HelpTopic	Displays help for the Fractal Lab.
WMLButtonUp	Detects that the user has requested a zoom and resets the coordinates based on the zoom rectangle.
GetClassName	Returns "WFractalWindow".
GetWindowClass	Sets the icon for this lab to the proper icon.

Chapter

3

Emergent

BEHAVIOR

PHEROMONE	Chemical substance secreted by animals that can influence other animals. Langton's *vants* left pheromone trails for other vants to follow.
L-SYSTEMS	Computer-generated plants that look a lot like real plants.
BOIDS	Bird-like computer creatures created by Craig Reynolds after watching the flocking behavior of real birds.
VANTS	A computer program written by Chris Langton that models the behavior of real-life ants.

As discussed in Chapter 1, "Introduction to Complexity," complexity is "the study of emergent behavior exhibited by interacting components operating at the threshold between stability and chaos." In Chapter 2, "Stability, Chaos, and Complexity," you explored stability and chaos. In this chapter you continue your exploration of complexity by focusing on the emergent behavior of interactive systems. As mentioned in Chapter 1, the behavior of individual components is seldom surprising and is best studied using traditional science. It is only when these individual components interact with each other and influence each other through these interactions that the system as a whole can begin to exhibit complex, emergent behavior. This chapter begins the examination of emergent behavior with a closer look at the interacting systems that produce this behavior.

Computer programs provide good examples of individual, independent components displaying predictable, noncomplex behavior and of systems of interacting components displaying emergent behavior. It is fairly easy to write a computer program that performs a large number of actions sequentially. Do step one, then step two, then step three, and so on. Traditional mainframe batch programs operate very much in this manner, with the addition of a few loops to repeat a series of steps and branches that allow the computer to jump to a new set of instructions based on some type of condition. These types of computer programs act as individual entities and do not interact with users or other programs. Their behavior is very predictable and is not complex.

In the 1980s, interactive computer programs became the rage. No longer could the computer simply speed along some predefined track created by the programmer. In interactive programs, the computer must interact with a human. The computer's actions are largely dictated by the whims of the person sitting at the keyboard. Writing computer programs became much more difficult, and exhaustively testing them for every possible scenario became impossible. In an attempt to manage the difficulty, an entirely new programming paradigm was invented. With *event-driven programming*, used by virtually all major graphical user interfaces, a program can be designed to respond to events that occur in response to a user action (mouse movement, key press, and so on). Those of you who have used Microsoft Windows or Macintosh applications can attest to the fact that event-driven interactive computer programs work. If you have ever tried to program a Microsoft Windows or Macintosh application, you know that writing and testing these programs is an extremely difficult task.

REAL WORLD

Potential. The stock market is one good example of an interacting system that exhibits emergent behavior. It certainly seems possible that someone could build a computer program (perhaps using the genetic programming approaches described in Chapter 6 "Programming with Genetic Algorithms") that would take as input stock and other financial and attitudinal data and allow a computer to predict the behavior of the market as a whole and of individual classes of stocks.

What happens when the computer program no longer interacts with a single external entity, but is forced to interact with hundreds, or thousands, or *millions* of external entities simultaneously? From the perspective of an individual program, or program element, the behavior may begin to approach chaos. It becomes impossible to make significant long-term predictions of behavior because of uncertainties in the initial conditions. We might expect a system with these components to also exhibit chaotic, unpredictable behavior, but it doesn't.

REAL WORLD

Actual. One exciting use of emergent behavior is as a means of identifying fundamental rules and principles that may underlie actual behavior of real-world systems. For example, have you ever wondered why heavy traffic often produces miles of very slow traffic followed by miles during which you move along quite rapidly, with no apparent reason for either the slow or the fast areas? A simple computer model of drivers (with reaction times, comfortable following distances, and so on programmed in) produced the identical behavior in a computer. This computer model could then be used to determine exactly how much traffic was needed to produce this type of traffic phenomenon under varying road and lighting conditions.

In many cases, these systems begin to exhibit emergent behavior. As described in Chapter 1, emergent behavior is behavior that was not programmed in from the beginning, but rather emerged as a complex system operated. It is important to differentiate between emergent and unpredictable behavior. *Emergent behavior* is behavior that was not intentionally programmed in from the beginning and that was somehow surprising to the program's creator. Once observed, the behavior can often be quite predictable, however. One approach to tapping into this emergent behavior is through the use of Genetic Programming, a topic I'll address in Chapter 6. To get a look at this phenomenon firsthand, let's play with one of the all-time classic examples of emergent behavior, the computer program Boids.

A Classic in Emergent Behavior—Boids

Craig Reynolds first became interested in modeling complex movements in animals while working as a computer animator. Reynolds used to eat lunch with friends by a cemetery near Culver City, California, and watch as blackbirds flocked, speculating on how difficult a task it would be to get computer creatures to flock in the same manner. The more Reynolds studied the birds, the more convinced he became that the complex phenomenon we call flocking must be based on a small number of rules each bird individually applied. Over time, he developed three key rules:

1. The birds need to look around their local area and decide where most other birds are, then try to head in that direction.

2. The birds need to look at their neighbors and try to match velocity with them.

3. The birds need to avoid bumping into each other and obstacles in their path.

Reynolds created a program, called Boids, for the 1987 SIGGRAPH computer graphics convention. The program displayed the movements of several birdlike creatures (boids) on the screen. Each boid acted as an individual, following the key rules mentioned in the preceding list. After much fine tuning, the boids began to exhibit amazingly birdlike behavior. They would quickly form a flock and maintain the integrity of the flock as they flew around. When confronted with obstacles, the flock would sometimes split, fly around the obstacle, and reunite on the other side. In one well-known run, an individual boid was trapped and ended up flying into a column. The stunned boid halted for an instant, recovered, and sped up

Enter the COMPLEXITY LAB

to rejoin the flock. None of the flocking behavior had been explicitly programmed by Reynolds. Rather, the behavior of the flock emerged as a result
of the simultaneous interactions between the individual boids. Ornitholo-
gists studied Reynolds' Boids program and were so impressed with the
lifelike behavior of the flock that they hypothesize real-life birds may be
following a set of internal rules very similar to Reynolds' computer rules.

My implementation of Boids follows the same general concept as Reynolds'
program but is otherwise completely new. Reynolds controlled the perceived center of mass of the flock and thus was able to move the flock in a
pattern of his choice. I chose to allow the individual boids to determine their
own direction and perceived center of mass, to see if flocking behavior was
still observed. To run this version of the classic program, select New Boid
from the Complexity program's File menu. A window similar to Figure 3.1
is displayed.

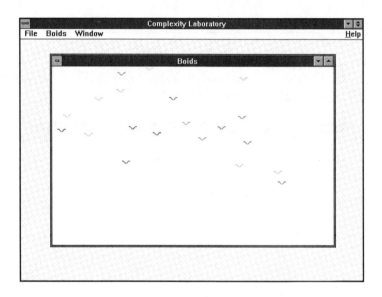

Figure 3.1.
Boids initial
window.

Selecting Boids, then Setup from the Boids drop-down menu displays the
dialog box shown in Figure 3.2. You can use this dialog box to control the
number of boids displayed on the screen and the speed at which the boids
are moved. (The speed is initially set to 0, the value for the fastest possible
speed.)

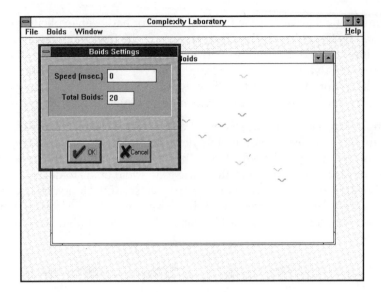

Figure 3.2.
Boids Setup dialog box.

Select Boids, then Run from the Boids drop-down menu. The boids begin to move according to the rules for boid behavior. Over time, the individual boids begin to form into one or more flocks (see Figure 3.3).

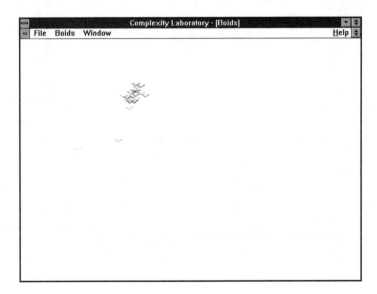

Figure 3.3.
Flocking behavior in boids.

Enter the COMPLEXITY LAB

To put obstacles in the path of the flock of boids, use the left mouse button to drag a rectangle on the screen (Figure 3.4). One example of emergent behavior I observed while playing with my boid flocks is the fact that boids tend to hang around in the area of the screen with the least obstacles. Apparently these boids like to have a bit of maneuvering room when flying!

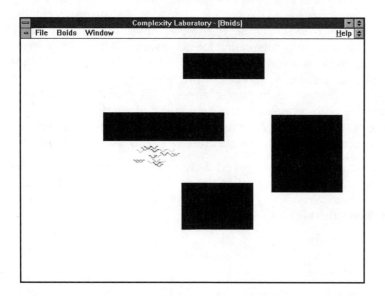

Figure 3.4.
Adding obstacles on the screen.

Other Examples of Emergent Behavior

It seems plausible that emergent behavior is all around us, staring us in the face every day. Chris Langton wrote an incredibly simple program called Vants (Virtual Ants) that may explain how ants are able to quickly devour that potato chip you dropped during your picnic. Langton's vants are V-shaped objects that move in the direction of the point of the V. Like boids, each individual vant followed a simple set of rules:

1. If a vant moved into a blank cell on the screen, it continued in the same direction.
2. If the cell was blue, the vant changed it to yellow and turned right.
3. If the cell was yellow, the vant changed it to blue and turned left.

When Langton placed one vant on the screen, ho-hum—but when he added several vants, he observed behavior strikingly similar to that of real ants. The vants left a type of pheromone trail that allowed other vants to follow them and eventually build a spiraling path.

Another example of emergent behavior that may model the way real-world systems develop is found in graphical plants created using a technique first described by Aristid Lindenmayer and Prezemyslaw Prusinkiewicz. These computer-generated plants, called L-Systems, start with a single stem or seed. They then use a series of very simple, localized rules of behavior to control the shape of each new cell during plant growth. The result is amazingly lifelike plants with branches, leaves, flowers, and so on. These plants are amazing both because of their complexity, given the simple rules, and because of their uncanny resemblance to real-life plants. L-Systems are often used by computer artists to create artificial plants, gardens, and forests.

The fundamental rules that govern L-Systems are quite simple. You begin with a seed value consisting of one or more letters from a finite alphabet, such as a, b, c.... You apply a series of production rules to this seed. The production rules take the form of

$$a \rightarrow ab$$
$$b \rightarrow bbc$$
$$c \rightarrow a$$

Finally, you interpret the resulting string. For example:

$$a \rightarrow \text{Turn right 30 degrees; draw four pixels}$$
$$b \rightarrow \text{Turn left 30 degrees; draw four pixels}$$
$$c \rightarrow \text{Draw eight pixels}$$

With the right combination of production rules and drawing rules, you end up with ferns, trees, and various other plantlike shapes. Amazingly, there is some evidence that similar rules dictate actual plant growth. For example, the rules that govern *anabaena catenula* (blue-green algae) are

1. The alphabet consists of specialized cells, called *heterocysts* (h) and generalized cells (g).
2. Generalized cells come in two flavors, small (g_s) and large (g_l).

Enter the COMPLEXITY LAB

3. The production rules observed in nature are

$$h \rightarrow \emptyset \; // \text{do not divide}$$
$$g_s \, g_l \rightarrow g_s \, g_l \, g_l$$
$$g_l \, g_s \rightarrow g_l \, g_l \, g_s$$
$$g_l \rightarrow g_l \, g_s$$
$$g_s \rightarrow g_s \, g_l$$

These simple rules allow a computer-based L-System model to accurately predict the growth of *anabaena catenula* algae.

REAL WORLD

Actual. Studying the behavior of systems rather than individual components allowed researchers to discover the principle of *autocatalytic sets*, in which the members of a chain of chemicals each help in the formation of the next member in the chain and the last member ultimately helps in the formation of the first. These autocatalytic sets quickly self-reinforce to produce a large number of each of the chemicals in the chain. Understanding this system-level emergent behavior may enable us to better understand things such as the emergence of life on earth from an environment rich in both chemicals and catalysts.

Scientists have wondered for ages how individual cells differentiate into the various parts of your body. You started as a single cell that divided into two cells, then four, then eight, and so on. Why did some of those cells become your hands, while others became your eyes? How does the genetic code in each cell enable a new, properly formed living organism to develop? The answer may lie in emergent behavior similar to the computer generated L-System plants. If a limited set of finite rules, each dependent only on localized knowledge of the cell's immediate vicinity, can allow a computer simulation to create lifelike plants, doesn't it seem possible that a similarly simple set of rules encoded in the genetic algorithm of each cell in a human body can allow the cells to determine exactly what form they need to take? The overall blueprint for a human being never needs to exist, but rather is allowed to emerge from the complex interaction of many cells following a small number of rules that are each dependent on localized knowledge.

Practical Reasons for Studying Emergent Behavior in Complex Systems

Emergent behavior is more than just fun to watch. Many complex, real-world systems exhibit behavior that has fascinated and baffled scientists for hundreds of years. Approaches to understanding this behavior by observing either the group or individuals within the group have often been fruitless. An alternate tool is now available. Scientists can create a computer model of the complex system and play with different relatively simple, plausible rules for interaction. When the observed behavior of the simulated system matches the observed behavior of the real-world system for a wide variety of scenarios, it might be possible that the rules of the computer-programmed, simulated systems at least partially match those of the nature-programmed, real-world systems. In some cases, specific real-world experiments can then be used to test the hypothesis.

When the simulated system closely parallels the behavior of the real-world system, another possibility arises. Scientists can alter the environment within the simulated system and observe the behavior of the system. If the model of the real-world system is a valid one, the scientists can reasonably expect the real-world system to behave in a fashion similar to the simulated system when confronted with the same environmental changes. In this way, it is possible to predict the behavior of complex, real-world systems using computer simulations of those systems.

In some cases, the technique of using simple interactions to create complex, emergent behavior can be put to practical use outside the modeling realm. You've seen one example in this chapter, where L-Systems are used by computer artists to create lifelike plants with relatively little programming. Another example with immediate ramifications is in the area of robotics.

On the MIT campus you will find the Mobile Robot (MOBOT) group at MIT's Artificial Intelligence Laboratory. There, researchers are building robots with many computer chips, each designed to perform specialized, localized processing. Instead of a massive central processing unit controlling every aspect of the robot's behavior, these robots move using simple rules based on very localized inputs. One example is Genghis, a foot-long robot that more nearly resembles a large cockroach than anything else.

Enter the COMPLEXITY LAB

When Genghis comes to life, he begins to make his way across the room. Place a phone book in his path and he stops, climbs on top, climbs down the other side, and continues his walk. No computer ever told Genghis how to climb over a phone book. Walking, avoiding obstacles, and climbing over obstacles are all emergent behaviors.

REAL WORLD

Potential. One of the best potential uses for emergent behavior is in the field of robotics. Instead of trying to design a super-smart central processor for the robot that coordinates every sensor and movement, perhaps robots should be designed to use numerous distributed processors that take localized actions yet contribute to the more global emergent behavior of the robot itself. The resultant robot should be very adaptable, economical, and able to respond quickly to a wide range of circumstances. Robots with these characteristics have many more potential uses, including acting as guards, autonomous explorers of hostile areas such as other planets and the ocean floor, and performing household chores such as vacuuming.

Small robots similar to Genghis might eventually keep your house clean, explore Mars, or inspect remote areas. Microscopic *nanobots* using similar principles might search out and kill cancer cells from within your bloodstream.

Emergent Behavior as an Example of Artificial Thought

Can a computer program be alive? Perhaps so, in the way a virus or bacteria is alive. It can certainly reproduce—computer viruses have spread around the world in days. It has an encoding that uniquely identifies it. It can have sex during the reproductive process, as demonstrated in the genetic programs in Chapter 6. It can respond to its environment, learn, die—in short, a computer program can embody most, if not all, of what we call life.

Can it be alive and intelligent at the human level? Probably not, using current approaches to designing programs. The best we can hope to achieve is a very limited intelligence, or a façade that appears intelligent in the right circumstances. I believe it is likely, however, that true artificial thought on a par with human thought can ultimately be created, using approaches that emerge from the study of complexity theory. I believe that we will never be able to program artificial thought into a computer, but that it will eventually be possible to create a network of small programs, perhaps each running on its own CPU, capable of exhibiting emergent behavior that we can classify as artificial thought on the same level of intelligence as yours and mine.

Further, I believe that artificial thought researchers can never successfully preprogram the behavior of the complex system as a whole, nor will they be able to fully program the individual elements of the system. I believe that artificial thought will eventually emerge from a complex system of interacting programs, each of which in turn exhibits emergent behavior from a localized set of inputs and operating rules. If you're wondering where the localized set of operating rules will come from for each element, perhaps the answer is found in our discussion of genetic programming in Chapter 6. First, though, we need to study cellular automata to better understand the essence of complex behavior and to further explore the fine line between chaos and stability.

Suggested Further Reading

Complexity: The Emerging Science at the Edge of Order and Chaos. M. Mitchell Waldrop, Simon & Schuster, NY, 1992. This is the book on complexity that started my initial interest in the topic. A fun read with a broad coverage of the people and events that got complexity theory to where it is today.

Artificial Life: The Quest for a New Creation. Steven Levy, Pantheon Books, NY, 1992. An excellent general overview of many aspects of complexity with an emphasis on emergent behavior that begins to gray the line between death and life. More than any other book I've ever read, this one is a conversation starter when you read it around others.

Designing Autonomous Agents: Theory and Practice from Biology to Engineering and Back. Edited by Pattie Maes, MIT/Elsevier, NY, 1991. A collection of academic papers on related topics. If you're a researcher getting heavily into this area, this book might be a good starting point for your research, but it's a bit too academic for general audiences.

For Programmers Only

The Boids Lab uses three classes. `WBoidWindow` and `WBoidDialog` are the lab's main window and Setup dialog handler. The class `WBoid` represents an individual boid and is used by the `WBoidWindow` to create a flock of boids.

The basic rules I attempted to implement in the computer were as follows:

1. The boids should avoid walls (rectangles) and each other.
2. The boids should avoid standing still, and should prefer to fly fast (fast is more fun to watch than slow).
3. The boids should seek the center of mass of nearby boids.
4. The boids should attempt to match velocity with the closest boid.

The boids' positions are updated individually. For each boid, I begin with a matrix of integers that represent potential locations to move to. I set each cell in the matrix to zero, which indicates a neutral location. If a cell in the matrix corresponds to hitting a rectangle on the screen, I set the cell to a very large negative number, indicating a poor choice for a move. If another boid already occupies a cell, I set the cell to a negative number that is somewhat smaller than the number for hitting a rectangle but still not desirable. Given a choice between hitting another boid and hitting a wall, my boids will hit the other boid. I then set the current location of the boid to a negative number, encouraging the boid to fly somewhere, and set the closest neighbor locations to a slightly smaller negative number to encourage the boid to fly fast (move farther each time).

To encourage the boid to seek the apparent center of mass, I plot a line from the boid's position to all nearby boids, increasing the cell values along this imaginary line. Finally, I implement velocity-matching by having the boid store a goal X and Y displacement (corresponding to a new cell position) and increasing the value of the cell at its goal location. Each boid will attempt to match velocities with its neighbors by taking on the closest neighbor's goal value. Figure 3.5 contains a flow chart that summarizes the algorithm I've just described.

The Boid Lab uses a very simple transfer buffer to communicate with its Setup dialog box.

```
// Transfer Buffer Used by WBoidDialog
struct BoidTransfer
{
        char Rate [6];
        char Boids [6];
        BoidTransfer ()
```

```
{
        strcpy (Rate, "0");
        strcpy (Boids, "20");
    };
};
```

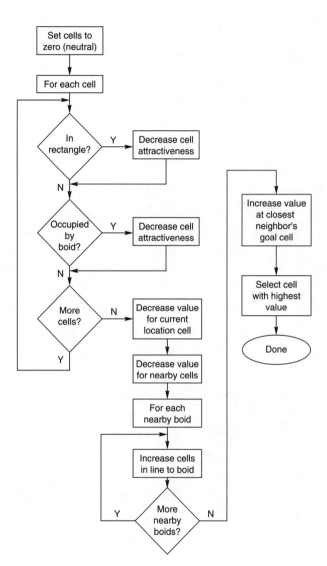

Figure 3.5.
*A summary of the
described algorithm,
in flow chart form.*

WBoidDialog

Figure 3.6 summarizes the WBoidDialog class design, and Table 3.1 describes the class member functions. This class is very simple and is used to support the Boid Setup dialog box.

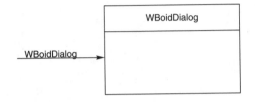

Figure 3.6.
WBoidDialog class design.

```
WBoidDialog(PTWindowsObject Parent,
            struct BoidTransfer*);
```

Table 3.1. WBoidDialog Member Function Descriptions

Member Function	Description
WBoidDialog	Constructor.

WBoidWindow

Figure 3.7 illustrates the class design for the WBoidWindow class. The member functions for the class are described in Table 3.2.

Table 3.2. WBoidWindow Member Function Descriptions

Member Function	Description
WBoidWindow	Constructor.
~WBoidWindow	Destructor.
ResetAll	Initializes all data members to default values.

Enter the COMPLEXITY LAB

Member Function	Description
SetupWindow	Performs window initialization functions.
Paint	Updates the contents of the window on the display screen.
InitChoices	Helper function to initialize the next move matrix used to determine the boid's next position.
AvoidRectangles	Helper function used to decrement specific cells in the next move matrix if those cells are occupied by a rectangle.
AvoidOtherBoids	Helper function used to decrement specific cells in the next move matrix if those cells are occupied by another boid.
SeekCenterOfMass	Helper function to identify all nearby boids and increment next move matrix cells if they are between this boid and each of the other boids.
DDALine	Helper function used by SeekCenterOfMass to determine which next move matrix cells should be incremented in a straight line between this boid and a given other boid.
About	Handles the Boids Lab About dialog box.
Settings	Handles the Boids Lab Settings dialog box.
Update	Updates the position of some boids, with the exact number based on the CPUSpeed.
WMLButtonDown	Adds the user-specified rectangle to the list of rectangles to be avoided.
HelpTopic	Displays help on the Boids Lab.
GetClassName	Returns "WBoidWindow".
GetWindowClass	Used to specify the proper icon for the Boids Lab application.

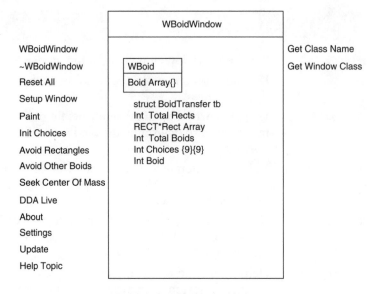

WBoidWindow		
WBoidWindow		Get Class Name
~WBoidWindow	WBoid	Get Window Class
Reset All	Boid Array{}	
Setup Window	struct BoidTransfer tb	
Paint	Int Total Rects	
Init Choices	RECT*Rect Array	
Avoid Rectangles	Int Total Boids	
Avoid Other Boids	Int Choices {9}{9}	
Seek Center Of Mass	Int Boid	
DDA Live		
About		
Settings		
Update		
Help Topic		

Figure 3.7.
*WBoidWindow
class design.*

```
WBoidWindow (PTWindowsObject Frame);
~WBoidWindow();

void ResetAll();

void SetupWindow();
LPSTR GetClassName();
void GetWindowClass(WNDCLASS &);
void Paint (HDC PaintDC, PAINTSTRUCT&ps);
void InitChoices();
void AvoidRectangles ();
void AvoidOther Boids ();
void SeekCenterOfMass ();
int DDALine (int X,int Y,int Inc);

void About (RTMessage)=
        [CM_FIRST+CM_About];
void Settings (RTMessage)=
        [CM_FIRST+CM_Setup];
void Update (RTMessage)=
        [WM_FIRST+WM_TIMER];
void WMLButtonUp (RTMessage)=
        [WM_FIRST+WM_LBUTTONUP];
void Help Topic ()=[CM_FIRST+CM_HelpTopic];
```

Enter the COMPLEXITY LAB

WBoid

Figure 3.8 illustrates the WBoid class design, and Table 3.3 describes each of the class member functions. This class encapsulates a single boid and is used by the WBoidWindow to create a flock of boids. The data members GoalX and GoalY are expressed in terms of a desired new location in the next move matrix rather than a location in the simulated world. In this sense, they correspond more to a desired velocity than to a goal position. The boid class declares the WBoidWindow class to be a friend to give that class access to its private data members.

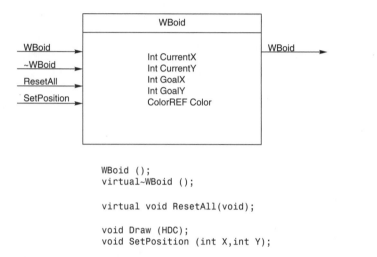

Figure 3.8.
WBoid class design.

```
WBoid ();
virtual~WBoid ();

virtual void ResetAll(void);

void Draw (HDC);
void SetPosition (int X,int Y);
```

Table 3.3. WBoid Member Function Descriptions

Member Function	Description
WBoid	Constructor.
~WBoid	Destructor.
ResetAll	Resets all data members to their default values.
SetPosition	Moves the boid to a new position.
Draw	Draws the boid using the exclusive OR pen and the boid's own color. Using the exclusive OR pen allows WBoidWindow to later redraw the boid at the same location to erase it.

Chapter

4

One-
Dimensional
CELLULAR
Automata

STATES	Values, which can be associated with each of a series of cells that make up a cellular automaton.
SELF-ORGANIZED CRITICALITY	The theory that many interacting systems naturally and inevitably evolve to a critical state existing at the edge of chaos and stability.
TRANSITION RULES	A collection of zero or more rules associated with each cellular automaton that determine how cells of the automaton make the transition between states.

Complex behavior is observed only at the transition between stability and chaos. In a real-world system, how can you tell where this transition region is? Exactly what happens as you approach it? This chapter explores the transition from stability, through complexity, to chaos. One-dimensional cellular automata are used to demonstrate the concept visually. In addition, I'll provide some evidence of forces that ensure that systems operating in this narrow complex region are not just possible but, in many cases, inevitable.

 REAL WORLD

Potential. It is my belief that successful species exist in the region between stability and chaos, adapting to new situations but not falling apart with seemingly random transitions. Further, it is my belief that many extinct species are extinct because they were not able to successfully remain in this narrow region, being forced from it by external circumstances such as the environment, internal difficulties, or other species. Perhaps better models of species behavior and interaction will allow us to better predict which species will become extinct in the future if we do not intervene, whether or not our intervention will help, and if it will help, what the best approach is to follow.

Cellular Automata

Cellular automata have been a staple of computer modeling since they were first invented by John von Neumann in the 1950s. A cellular automaton consists of a series of cells, each of which can take on a finite number of values, called *states*. For example, on a computer screen the cells are often colored based on their state. Associated with each cellular automaton is a collection of zero or more rules (called *transition rules*) that determine how cells of the automaton make the transition between states. A cellular automaton chugs along, making one transition at a time. During each transition, all cells are examined and potentially changed. For each cell, the rules determine its new state based on its current state and the states of neighboring cells. For example, one transition rule might say, "If the previous dot color is blue and there is a red cell to the left, then the new dot color is red."

Enter the COMPLEXITY LAB

Cellular automata can be one-dimensional, consisting of a single row of cell values that change with time. They can also be two-dimensional, consisting of a sort of extended checkerboard. In fact, they can have as many dimensions as you wish, using multi-dimensional matrices to keep track of each cell value. In this chapter I will focus on one-dimensional cellular automata.

The Tapestry Program

The Complexity Lab program, Tapestry, is an example of a one-dimensional cellular automaton. Each row of colored cells (which appear as dots on the screen) is determined based on the color patterns of the cells in the previous row. Tapestry is an example of an interacting system because each cell's new state is dependent on the current state of others. It is interesting to look at the various states of the Tapestry cellular automaton over time. Tapestry displays the state history by displaying the initial state on the top-most row of the screen, the second state on the second row, the third state on the third row, and so on. In effect, the screen shows the history of the cellular automaton, with the higher rows being older versions and the lower rows being newer versions.

Figure 4.1 shows the initial Tapestry screen, obtained by selecting Files, then New Tapestry from the Complexity Lab's main menu.

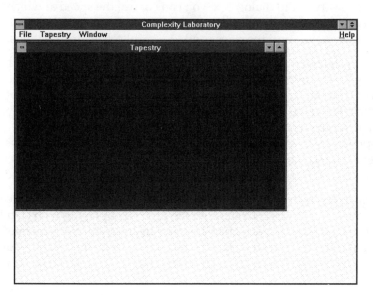

Figure 4.1.
The Tapestry initial screen.

CHAPTER FOUR   **One-Dimensional Cellular Automata**

Figure 4.2 shows the Tapestry Setup dialog box, accessed by selecting Setup from the Tapestry drop-down menu. This dialog box is used to control the characteristics of the cellular automaton that will be displayed.

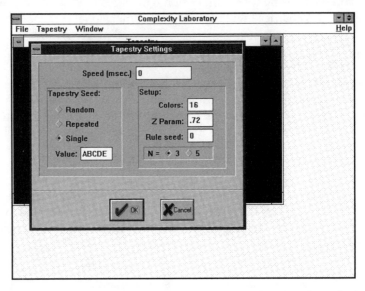

Figure 4.2.
The Tapestry Setup dialog box.

On the Tapestry Setup dialog box, you can control the speed at which Tapestry runs (0 msec is the fastest possible speed), the initial state of the cellular automaton, and the rules used to control cell state transitions.

The initial state of the cellular automaton is based on the settings in the Tapestry Seed group of the Tapestry Setup dialog box. The cellular automaton can be initialized with random values, with repeating instances of a user-specified value, or with a single, user-specified value. The user-specified value is entered as a series of letters A through Z, which correspond to states (colors) 1 through 26. You can specify as many as 10 different state/color values at one time for a repeating seed. The first letter in the user-specified series is used when initializing with a single seed.

When working with cellular automata, black cells are often called "dead" and colored cells "alive." To simplify the process of playing with stability, complexity, and chaos, I designed Tapestry to automatically generate cellular automaton transition rules with a user-specified probability of a cell

Enter the COMPLEXITY LAB

remaining alive. I called this the Z factor. Lower values of Z mean that cells are more likely to die, while higher values of Z mean they are more likely to stay alive (either by changing to a new color or by remaining the same color).

You can specify whether each transition rule should use the value of the current cell and its two nearest neighbors (N equal to 3 in the Setup group) or four nearest neighbors (N equal to 5). (In Tapestry, the row of cells acts as if the beginning is connected to the end, thereby producing a ring. In this way, the cells at the beginning and end of the row will have each other as neighbors during transitions.)

You can also determine whether the automatically generated rules should be truly random (rule seed equal to 0 in the Setup group) or pseudo-random with a repeatable sequence (rule seed not equal to 0). When the rule seed is truly random, no two runs of the Tapestry program are likely to be the same, even if all other setup parameters are identical. It is easier to experiment with the effects of changing the other setup parameters by using a nonrandom rule seed.

Finally, the Setup dialog box enables you to determine the number of possible states (colors) in the range of 1 through 255.

The Transition from Stability to Chaos

A note before we continue: Because the transition rules are randomly generated each time you exit the Setup dialog box, each run of the Tapestry program is unique. It may take several runs to obtain results similar to those illustrated in the following figures. To start a new run (rather than continue an existing run), you must enter the Setup dialog box and click the OK button.

Figure 4.3 shows what happens with a low value of Z (.2) and a random Tapestry seed. The cellular automaton starts in a random state (shown by the colors in the first few rows of the window) but quickly dies to a stable, dead state (shown by the remaining black rows). Figure 4.4 shows what happens with a high value of Z (.98) and a random Tapestry seed. The cellular automaton starts in a random state and remains chaotic. There is no order, or structure, in this system.

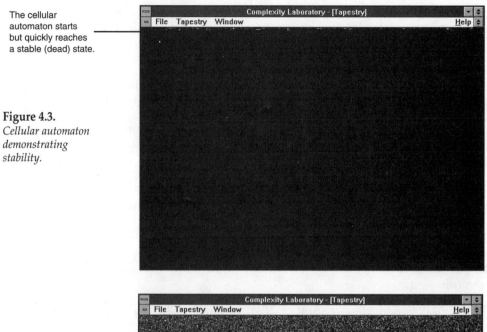

Figure 4.3.
*Cellular automaton
demonstrating
stability.*

Figure 4.4.
*Cellular automaton
demonstrating
chaos.*

In the transition region between stability and chaos, interesting complex
behavior can be observed. Figures 4.5 through 4.7 were produced with a
random Tapestry seed and the value of Z varying from .42 through .5.
Figure 4.5 is an example of an interesting, stable structure; the cellular
pattern slowly moves from left to right in an eternally repeating pattern.

Enter the COMPLEXITY LAB

Figure 4.6 is a good example of multiple repeating and stable patterns beginning to emerge. The cellular automaton in Figure 4.7, with a Z value of .5 and N set to 5, is clearly approaching chaos, but definite examples of underlying structures are also evident.

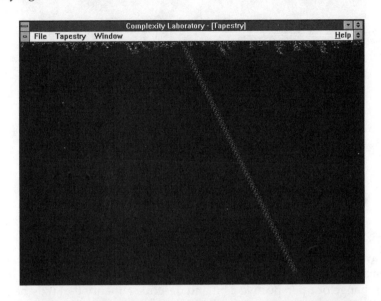

Figure 4.5.
Stable Tapestry pattern.

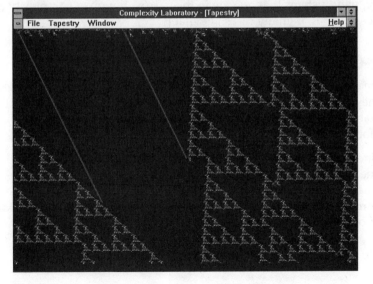

Figure 4.6.
A more complex, stable Tapestry pattern.

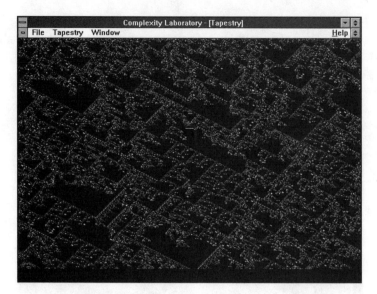

Figure 4.7.
Tapestry on the edge between stability and chaos.

Figures 4.3 through 4.7 can also be found in color in the Gallery.

You have been using the Tapestry program to explore the behavior of a system as it changes from stability, through complexity, to chaos. I would like to change our perspective a bit and describe a theory that may help to explain why systems that operate in the narrow region of complexity are not just possible but, in many cases, inevitable.

Self-Organized Criticality

Self-organized criticality is the theory that many interacting systems naturally and inevitably evolve to a critical state existing at the edge between chaos and stability. A popular example used to illustrate this concept is a pile of sand forming on a round tabletop.

Imagine a round table with a funnel suspended overhead. The funnel is designed to allow sand to be dropped on the table one grain at a time. Eventually, the table is completely covered with a pile of sand. As the pile of sand grows, it begins to display a consistent type of behavior that is known as self-organized criticality.

Enter the COMPLEXITY LAB

You can observe the self-organized critical behavior of the sand pile as each new grain of sand is added. Sometimes the added grain of sand manages to find a resting point with no sand falling off the table. Sometimes the added grain of sand dislodges other grains that dislodge other grains, eventually resulting in a stable configuration with no sand falling off the table. Sometimes the dislodged grains of sand eventually result in a few grains of sand falling off. Sometimes the single grain of sand results in an ever-increasing avalanche of sand, resulting in a large amount of sand falling off the table.

Over time, the sand pile will maintain a roughly constant slope and height. This constant slope and height of the sand pile is its critical state. If you attempt to change the slope by smoothing it out (placing the sand pile in a *sub-critical* state, the avalanches will be smaller until the pile grows to the critical state. If you carefully position the grains of sand one at a time, the *supercritical* pile will eventually produce an avalanche much larger than normal. Both subcritical and supercritical states are naturally forced to the exact critical state.

If you attempt to predict the results of adding one grain of sand to the table, you will quickly find that the problem exhibits the characteristics of chaos. For all practical purposes, it is impossible to predict the number of grains of sand that will be eventually dislodged by a particular single grain of sand. On the other hand, the sandpile exhibits structure because its grains of sand interlock. In addition, although it is not possible to predict the results of an individual action (dropping a single grain of sand), it *is* possible to predict the behavior of the system (the sandpile as a whole).

If you plotted the flow of sand off the table over time, you would see a graph that looks very erratic and has features of all durations. You can view the graph as being a complicated wave, or *signal*. The signal from the sand pile is called *flicker noise*. Flicker noise indicates a correlation between current system activities and past system activities. As a result, the existence of flicker noise suggests a system that is strongly influenced by past events. If no correlation exists between the current system activities and past events, the signal is random. Random signals are called *white noise*. Further, the magnitudes of the avalanches of sand, expressed in terms of the number of avalanches of sand that result in a particular number of grains of sand falling off the table, can be plotted in a histogram. If you do this, you will find that the number of trials that resulted in a particular number of grains of sand falling can be roughly expressed as

$$\frac{1}{s^a}$$

where

  s = the number of grains of sand that fell
  a = a constant that must be empirically derived

This equation is called a form of *power law*, and systems that follow this pattern are said to behave in accordance with a power law. Power laws can also be used to describe the behavior of such diverse natural phenomena as the energy released by earthquakes, the distribution of earthquake epicenters, and the distribution of objects such as mountains, galaxies, and vortices in turbulent fluids. In their paper "Self-Organized Criticality," Peter Bak and Kan Chen suggested that the presence of a power law distribution is evidence of self-organized criticality, that flicker noise is a temporal fingerprint of self-organized criticality, and that fractal structures can be viewed as snapshots that show the spatial fingerprint of a self-organizing critical system. They also demonstrate that the uncertainty in the behavior of self-organized critical systems grows much more slowly than it does in chaotic systems (because uncertainty increases according to a power law rather than an exponential law).

From our perspective, the sandpile example describes how an interacting system can be forced, inevitably and inexorably, to the exact critical point. I believe that the same is true of biological systems, which can best exist and survive in the narrow boundary of complexity found between chaos and stability.

Cellular Automata and Self-Reproducing Factories

The Holy Grail of cellular automata has always been an attempt to define rules that would allow a structure, represented by a certain pattern within the cells, to reproduce itself. Each state transition rule would allow the structure to build a closer and closer likeness, until eventually the copy was independent. Both structures could then begin building more copies. Many mathematicians have spent untold time (years, in some cases) trying to find the simplest possible set of rules that allows a cellular automaton structure to self-reproduce.

Enter the COMPLEXITY LAB

If you're like me, you may be inclined to something of a "so what" perspective on self-reproducing cellular automata. I was interested, however, in a similar concept that was at least partially inspired by research in this area. I'm referring to self-reproducing factories.

Suppose you could build an automated factory that included every step in the production cycle needed to make a copy of itself. It would need to include equipment to automatically mine and smelt the metal, fabrication robots, assembly robots, and so on. The automated factory would work and work, eventually ending up with an exact copy of itself. Both copies could then begin the process of building more automated factories. In this way, the number of automated factories would steadily increase until eventually the available raw materials were exhausted.

REAL WORLD

Actual. Medical researchers are looking at the transition from stability to chaos to try to better understand why some people suddenly find that their body completely fails, suffering massive infection, heart attacks, and so on. They believe that by studying the body as an interacting system, operating on the threshold of chaos and stability, they may better understand what forces the system into chaos (and hence, failure). This knowledge may allow them to predict, and ultimately prevent, this failure of the body to adjust.

On the surface, the idea is interesting but far-fetched. Suppose, however, we simplify the concept and extend it to less mechanical domains. In many ways, a nuclear chain reaction is a form of automated factory. Each fission reaction releases two neutrons that are then free to start two more fission reactions. Perhaps we can view biologic systems as nature's form of automated factory. Each virus, bacteria, plant, or person makes copies of itself, and these copies then make additional copies. What if we look beyond nature to man-made automated factories that involve natural-type creatures?

I read recently that scientists had developed a microbe that was genetically engineered to eat oil. An oil slick could be sprayed with these little oil-gobbling microbes, which would then begin to create copies of themselves (self-reproducing) while consuming oil in the process. The end result would be lots of oil eating microbes that eventually run out of resources (oil), leaving a clean ocean for you and me.

Self-reproducing factories are fascinating because, in many ways, you get lots of somethings (the factories) with very little initial investment (building one and turning it loose). If the factories are designed to produce a valuable commodity as a surplus of the production cycle, you have a very low cost way (in terms of human effort) to produce something. Unfortunately, automated factories also have their disadvantages. It's interesting to speculate what the results would be if those oil-eating microbes were introduced into the world's underground oil fields. Suppose someone developed a small oxygen-eating, automated factory and released it into the atmosphere?

In the next chapter I extend the concept of one-dimensional cellular automata to multiple dimensions and provide examples of how multidimensional cellular automata are applicable to some computer modeling problems. In addition, I introduce Life, a two-dimensional cellular automaton that is a classic computer program from the field of artificial life.

Suggested Readings

"Self-Organized Criticality," by Peter Bak and Kan Chen, *Scientific American*, January, 1991, pp. 46-53. An excellent introductory paper on the concept of self-organized criticality as it relates to complexity.

Complexity: Life at the Edge of Chaos, by Roger Lewin, Macmillan Publishing, 1992. A fun-to-read book with lots of storytelling emphasis and character development. A high-level view of complexity as found between stability and chaos.

Creating Artificial Life: Self Organization, by Edward Rietman, Windcrest/McGraw Hill, 1993. A short but advanced text on complexity, artificial life, and cellular automata, with a software disk included.

Enter the COMPLEXITY LAB

The Global Dynamics of Cellular Automata, by Andrew Wuensche and Mike Lesser, Addison-Wesley Publishing, 1992. A *tour de force* of one-dimensional cellular automata, with a tremendous number of beautiful and fascinating color photographs. A disk is included.

For Programmers Only

The Tapestry Lab program is implemented using two classes, `WTapestryWindow` and `WTapestryDialog`. As usual, the `WTapestryDialog` simply handles the setup dialog box for the class. Within the `WTapestryWindow`, the cellular automaton itself is implemented as an integer array the size of the window client area with each cell location corresponding to a pixel location. The Setup dialog box determines the range of values for each cell and the starting values when the lab initially runs.

Rather than have the transition rules specify the exact matching values required for each of the two (or four) neighboring cells (a large task when the cells might take on any value between 0 and 255), the transition rules specify an operation that occurs based on the sum of the current cell and the two or four neighboring cells' values. This total is first calculated for each cell, and then the transition values are applied to each cell to determine its new value. Pixel colors are selected based on the value in the cell.

The transfer buffer used for communication with the `WTapestryDialog` class is as follows:

```
struct TapestryTransfer
{
    char Rate [6];
    WORD Random;
    WORD Repeated;
    WORD Single;
    char Value [11];
    char Colors [6];
    char ZParam [6];
    char RuleSeed [6];
    WORD N3;
    WORD N5;
    TapestryTransfer ()
    {
        strcpy (Rate, "0");
        Random = FALSE;
        Repeated = FALSE;
        Single = TRUE;
        strcpy (Value, "ABCDEFGHIJ");
        strcpy (Colors, "16");
        strcpy (ZParam, ".72");
        strcpy (RuleSeed, "0");
        N3 = TRUE;
        N5 = FALSE;
    };
};
```

Enter the COMPLEXITY LAB

WTapestryDialog Class

Figure 4.8 illustrates the design of the WTapestryDialog class, and Table 4.1 describes the class member function.

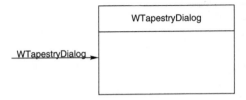

```
WTapestryDialog(PTWindowsObject Parent,
               struct TapestryTransfer*);
```

Figure 4.8.
*WTapestryDialog
class design.*

Table 4.1. WTapestryDialog Member Function Descriptions

Member Function	Description
WTapestryDialog	Constructor

WTapestryWindow Class

Figure 4.9 illustrates the design of the WTapestryWindow class, and Table 4.2 describes the class member functions.

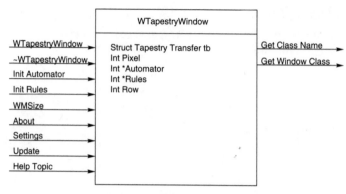

Figure 4.9.
WTapestryWindow
class design.

```
WTapestryWindow (PTWindowsObject Frame);
~WTapestryWindow();

void Init Automaton();
void Init Rules();

LPSTR GetClassName();
void GetWindowClass(WNDCLASS &);
void WMSize(RTMessage);

void About (RTMessage)=
        [CM_FIRST+CM_About];
void Settings (RTMessage)=
        [CM_FIRST+CM_Setup];
void Update (RTMessage)=
        [WM_FIRST+WM_TIMER];
void Help Topic ()=[CM_FIRST+CM_HelpTopic];
```

Table 4.2. WTapestryWindow Member Function Descriptions

Member Function	Description
WTapestryWindow	Constructor.
~WTapestryWindow	Destructor.
InitAutomaton	Initializes the automaton based on the user-specified initialization approach.
InitRules	Initializes the rules based on the user-specified value for Z.
WMSize	Responds to a Windows resize message.
About	Displays the Tapestry Lab About dialog box.
Settings	Displays the Tapestry Lab Setup dialog box.

Enter the COMPLEXITY LAB

Member Function	Description
Update	Calculates and displays all or part of a new row in the cellular automaton, based on the CPU speed.
HelpTopic	Displays help on the Tapestry Lab.
GetClassName	Displays "WTapestryWindow".
GetWindowClass	Used to set the icon for the Tapestry Lab window.

Chapter

5

Multi-
Dimensional

CELLULAR

Automata

THE GAME OF LIFE

The most famous example of Von Neumann's cellular automata.

LIFE

The possession of a capability to reproduce, to have variance within individuals, and to pass traits on to future generations through heredity.

GENETIC PROGRAMMING

Computer programs that evolve over time, reproducing themselves, inheriting behavior, and mutating.

In the previous chapter, I described and demonstrated one-dimensional cellular automata. Because cellular automata are so significant to the computer-based modeling that is often used to study complex systems, I will continue the discussion in this chapter by looking at multi-dimensional cellular automata. I will also expand the discussion of artificial life begun in Chapter 3, "Emergent Behavior," and use a classic computer program in the field of artificial life to illustrate both concepts.

Fun with Multi-dimensional Cellular Automata

In the previous chapter, I explained that a cellular automaton consists of a series of cells, each of which can take on a finite number of values, called *states*, and that the cellular automata chug along making one transition at a time. During each transition, each cell is examined and potentially changed as determined by a set of transition rules, which are based on the cell's current state and the state of its neighbors. I illustrated the concept with a one-dimensional cellular automaton, which was represented as a row of cells.

The concept can be easily extended to cover more than one dimension. You can picture a two-dimensional cellular automaton as a checkerboard, where each square corresponds to a single cell. This type of cellular automaton is often used to model geographic problems, where things move around on a surface. I used something similar to this concept when I implemented the Boids program in Chapter 3. A three-dimensional cellular automaton can be envisioned as a large cube made up of small sugar cubes, where each sugar cube represents a single cell. Although cellular automata of four dimensions and higher cannot be visualized as real-world objects, they are easy to visualize mathematically as a matrix with the desired number of dimensions. Each storage location in the matrix then corresponds to a cell.

Theoretical cellular automata are infinitely large in size for all dimensions. For example, a two-dimensional cellular automaton can be visualized as a plane that stretches forever in all directions. Most computers do not have the required amount of memory to store this (infinite) amount of information, and most users do not have the patience to wait an infinite amount of time to initialize it when their programs start! Computer modelers use one of two approaches to solve this dilemma. The first is to have an "edge of the world." The behavior of the cells at this edge will not be valid (or at least, not typical of the rest of the model) because they will have no neighboring cells on at least one side. Because the transition rules dictate changes based on the state of neighboring cells, the cells at the edge obviously have a major handicap.

Attractors Lab

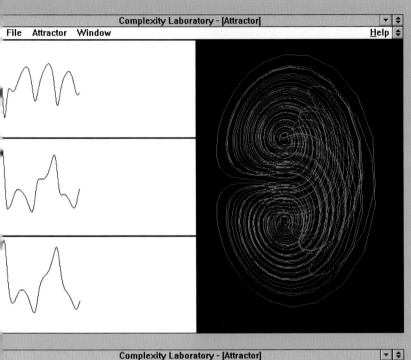

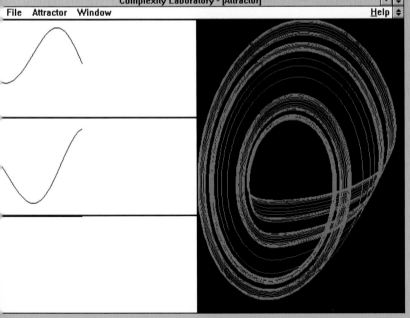

Enter various Julian and Lorenz equations in the Attractor Lab to generate a wide variety of stable attractors, including point attractors, inward spirals toward a point at infinity, outward spirals toward infinity, circular orbits, and two types of strange attractors. Figure at top shows an example of a Lorenz attractor and figure at bottom shows a Julian attractor. The Attractor Lab is discussed in Chapter 2, "Stability, Chaos, and Complexity."

Fractals Lab

In the top figure you begin with an initial Mandelbrot fractal created in the Fractals Lab. As you zoom in, it should begin to simplify (the dotted boxes in the figures show the area being zoomed).

To experiment yourself, start with a Mandelbrot set, then use the mouse to drag a rectangle over areas you would like to explore.

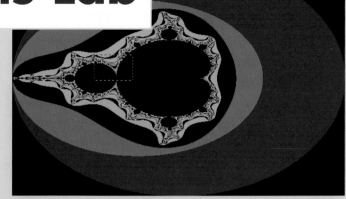

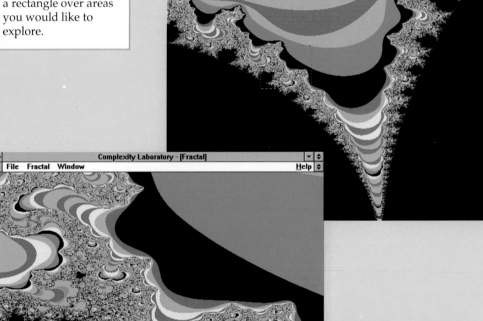

Mice in a Maze Lab

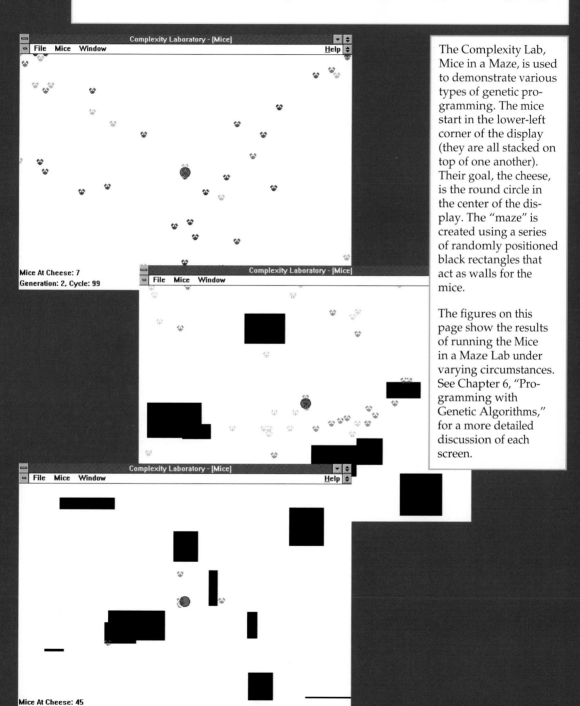

The Complexity Lab, Mice in a Maze, is used to demonstrate various types of genetic programming. The mice start in the lower-left corner of the display (they are all stacked on top of one another). Their goal, the cheese, is the round circle in the center of the display. The "maze" is created using a series of randomly positioned black rectangles that act as walls for the mice.

The figures on this page show the results of running the Mice in a Maze Lab under varying circumstances. See Chapter 6, "Programming with Genetic Algorithms," for a more detailed discussion of each screen.

Additional Shareware Programs on the Disk

The figures on this page show additional shareware programs that are on the accompanying disk. The larger two illustrate two different perspectives of the same Mandelbrot fractal in the program, Mandelbrot. The smaller two figures show screens from The Game of Life and Galaxy. These programs are discussed in Appendix B.

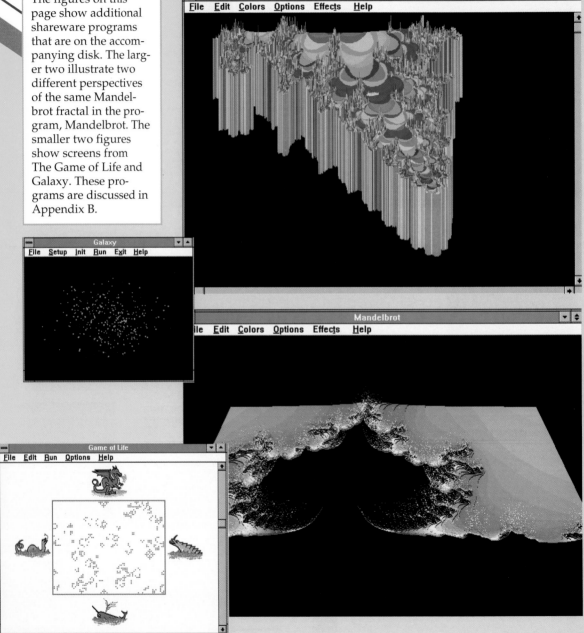

An alternate approach is to connect one side of the world to the other. Figure 5.1 illustrates this concept for one- and two-dimensional cellular automata. In the one-dimensional case, the result is a ring. The first cell in the model is considered to be next to the last cell. In the two-dimensional case, the result is a donut shape called a *toroid*. In the toroid, the first and last cells are adjacent and the top and bottom cells are adjacent. In Boids, the boids themselves move on a toroid. As they leave the top of the screen they reappear on the bottom and, as they leave one side, they reappear on the other. To simplify my programming task, however, I used the simpler approach of not seeing "around the world" when I implemented the behavior of looking for nearby boids. The program, Life, which is discussed in this chapter, contains a two-dimensional cellular automaton that has been implemented as a toroid.

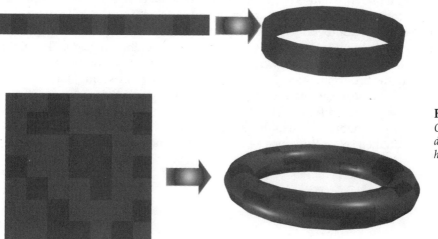

Figure 5.1.
One- and two-dimensional edge handling.

Life in a Computer

If you were a mathematics student in the late 1960s, there is a good chance that you wiled away more than a few hours sitting at a coffee table playing a game that involved placing and removing small playing pieces (often beads from a necklace) on a grid. The game was called Life, and it is the most famous example of Von Neumann's cellular automata.

Although human players moved the game pieces, they had no control over the position of the pieces. These positions were determined completely by the transition rules of the cellular automaton itself. The rules were simple.

- If a bead is in a cell, the cell is called alive. Cells with no beads are considered dead.
- Each cell has eight neighbors, four on the sides and four on the diagonals.
- If a cell is alive and has two or three neighbors, it will stay alive. It will starve if there are more than three and die of loneliness if there are less than two.
- If a cell is dead and has exactly three neighbors, it will be "born" and become alive.

As computers became available, it wasn't long before someone implemented Life on a computer. The program quickly became a classic of computer science and is included in the Complexity Lab as Life. Figure 5.2 (also contained in the Color Gallery) shows a sample run. A cell's color is based on the number of neighboring cells that are alive. Colors are selected from a pallet that is randomized each time you run the program. The initial state of the Life screen is also randomized each time you run the program. To run the program, select File, then New Life from the Complexity Lab's main menu. You can then select Run from the Life drop-down menu. To start over with a different initial configuration, select Setup from the Life drop-down menu, then exit the Setup dialog box by clicking the OK button. You can then select Run once again to start the new game running.

Enter the COMPLEXITY LAB

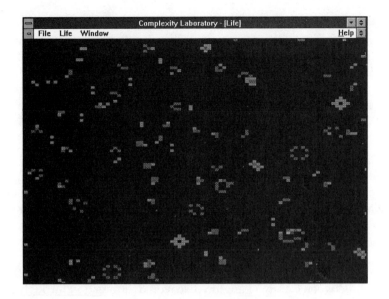

Figure 5.2.
A sample run of the game of Life.

The Game of Life

John Horton Conway, an eccentric but brilliant mathematician, studied the game of Life extensively in the late 1960s and early 1970s. He observed that some cells tended to settle into stable, unchanging patterns. He and his friends named these patterns after their appearance—block, ship, beehive, canoe, and pond. Other cells became stable oscillators, which he called blinkers, clocks, toads, and traffic lights. Occasionally, however, he observed more complex life forms. One example was R Pentomino, an arrangement of five cells shaped roughly like the letter *R*. This shape would change into a wide variety of unpredictable patterns, occasionally exploding into multiple objects. He also observed some shapes that moved steadily across the screen. These were called gliders. You might want to try several runs of Life in the Complexity Lab and attempt to do your own classifications of stable and oscillating shapes. In the meantime, watch for those elusive gliders.

One researcher who studied cellular automata (including Life) was Stephen Wolfram, a physics whiz-kid at Caltech. Wolfram contended that sets of cellular automata transition rules fall into one of four categories. Class I rules, often called doomsday rules, result in the system rapidly moving to a dead state for any initial configuration. Class II rules are somewhat more interesting, resulting in a combination of static and periodically oscillating blobs. These blobs are the stable attractors discussed in Chapter 2, "Stability, Chaos, and Complexity." Class III rules produce so much change that the screen seems to boil with activity. These are the chaotic systems. Finally, Class IV rules produce structures that exhibited interesting emergent behavior such as propagation, division, and recombination.

Chris Langton studied these four classes of cellular automata in an attempt to isolate why some sets of rules produced one class of behavior while others produced a different one. He eventually discovered a tuning parameter, which he called *lambda*, that allowed him to automatically generate cellular automaton rules that produced a particular class of behavior. Langton defined lambda as the probability of a given cell being alive in the next step. When lambda was set to 0, Langton could generate Class I automata. When lambda was set close to .5, he could generate Class III automata. Between 0 and .5 Langton discovered a transition through Class II automata to Class IV automata. (Above .5 the process was a mirror image of behavior below .5, with 1.0 resulting in all cells being alive rather than dead.) The magic number for two-dimensional cellular automata (resulting in the most complex behavior) seemed to be a lambda value of about .27, the approximate value for the game of Life. Once again, we see an example of the transition of complex systems from static, to stable, through complex, and then to chaotic. The Z factor that you set in the Tapestry program (described in the previous chapter) is roughly equivalent to Langton's lambda factor, although it goes from 0 (doomsday) to 1 (chaos).

Many people find watching Life to be almost hypnotic as it evolves on the computer screen. The feeling is somewhat akin to that of watching fish swim in a fish tank. The small creatures on the screen seem almost alive, which brings us to an interesting question: Is it possible to create life on the computer?

Is It Alive?

To decide if it is possible to create life on a computer, we must first agree on a working definition of life. Webster's dictionary defines life as "that property of plants and animals (ending at death and distinguishing them from inorganic matter) which makes it possible for them to take in food, get energy from it, grow, and so forth." I find this definition somewhat vague and unsatisfying. In the Encyclopedia Britannica, Carl Sagan claims that "there is no generally accepted definition of life." Should we define life in terms of the physical structure of the organism, such as requiring protein and water? This seems ludicrous, because it rules out many creatures that could live in the universe but be based on a totally different physical structure. For that matter, it rules out viruses on the earth.

Suppose we define life in terms of intelligence. How can we know when something is intelligent? Ants seem intelligent, but are they, like Chris Langton's vants, simply following a few preprogrammed instructions? Are bacteria intelligent? If they are, couldn't you argue that your microwave oven is intelligent, albeit with a different purpose in life? What about plants? Are they intelligent in any meaningful sense of the word as far as we can detect?

An increasingly accepted definition of life is the possession of a capability to reproduce, to have variance within individuals, and to pass traits on to future generations through heredity. All creatures that we could consider alive, from the lowest bacteria to a human being, contain DNA as the fundamental basis for reproduction, variation, and heredity. Nothing that we would intuitively consider not alive has those characteristics—nothing, that is, except some man-made computer programs.

One of the hottest fields in computer science today is genetic programming. These computer programs evolve over time, reproducing themselves, inheriting behavior, and mutating. They exhibit behavior that their original programmer never envisioned, and they operate in fashions that cannot be clearly explained, even by their creator. In a very real sense, they may just possibly be alive. This is the topic of our next chapter.

Suggested Reading

"Mathematical Games: The Fantastic Combinations of John Conway's New Solitaire Game Life," by Martin Gardner, *Scientific American*, October 1970, pp. 112-17. A good article describing the game of Life.
"Cellular Automata as Models of Complexity," by Stephen Wolfram, *Physica* 10D (1984), pp. 1-35. A good overview of cellular automata.
"Computer Software in Science and Mathematics," by Stephen Wolfram, *Scientific American*, September 1984, pp. 188-203. Another good overview article that covers cellular automata.

For Programmers Only

Two classes implement the Life Lab. The `WLifeDialog` class handles the Setup dialog box, and the `WLifeWindow` class handles the main window and all of the calculations. The cellular automaton itself is implemented as a 100 × 100 matrix of Boolean values (occupied or not). The matrix is a toroid, in that the value at 0 is considered to be next to the value at 100 in both directions. This matrix is then sized to cover the window's client area. Cells are colored based on the number of neighboring cells. The transfer buffer used to communicate with the Life Lab Setup dialog box is trivial, consisting of simply the Rate (or Speed) field.

```
struct LifeTransfer
{
     char Rate [6];
};
```

WLifeDialog

Figure 5.3 illustrates the class design for the `WLifeDialog` class, and Table 5.1 describes the single member function.

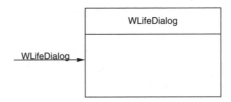

Figure 5.3.
WLifeDialog
class design.

```
WLifeDialog(PTWindowsObject Parent,
            struct LifeTransfer*);
```

Table 5.1. `WLifeDialog` Member Function Description

Member Function	Description
WLifeDialog	Constructor

WLifeWindow

Figure 5.4 illustrates the design of the `WLifeWindow` class, and Table 5.2 describes each of the class member functions.

Enter the COMPLEXITY LAB

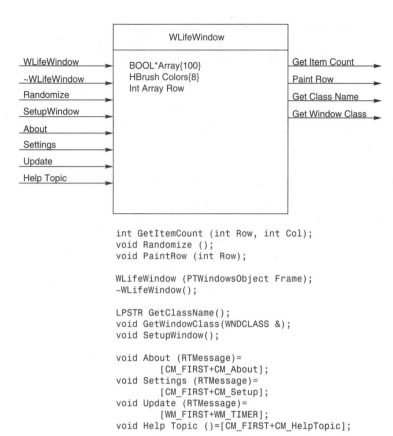

```
int GetItemCount (int Row, int Col);
void Randomize ();
void PaintRow (int Row);

WLifeWindow (PTWindowsObject Frame);
~WLifeWindow();

LPSTR GetClassName();
void GetWindowClass(WNDCLASS &);
void SetupWindow();

void About (RTMessage)=
        [CM_FIRST+CM_About];
void Settings (RTMessage)=
        [CM_FIRST+CM_Setup];
void Update (RTMessage)=
        [WM_FIRST+WM_TIMER];
void Help Topic ()=[CM_FIRST+CM_HelpTopic];
```

Figure 5.4.
WLifeWindow class design.

Table 5.2. `WLifeWindow` Member Function Descriptions

Member Function	Description
WLifeWindow	Constructor.
~WLifeWindow	Destructor.
Randomize	Randomizes the automaton array.
SetupWindow	Performs window setup functions.
About	Displays the Life Lab About dialog box.
Settings	Displays the Life Lab Settings dialog box.

continues

Table 5.2. continued

Member Function	Description
Update	Updates some cell values, with the number updated based on CPU speed.
HelpTopic	Displays help for the Life Lab.
GetItemCount	For a given cell, determines the number of neighbors with a live cell.
PaintRow	Draws a single row of the matrix.
GetClassName	Returns "WLifeWindow".
GetWindowClass	Used to set the icon for the window to the proper icon for the Life Lab.

Enter the COMPLEXITY LAB

Chapter

6

PROGRAMMING

with Genetic
Algorithms

STATE	Status. A finite state machine can exist in one or more states and has some way of knowing its current state.
RED QUEEN LEARNING	A form of competitive learning in which both the proponent and the opponent are continuously improving.
BUCKET BRIGADE	An algorithm in which rewards are effectively passed from the external environment to a long chain of rules that results in the reward being given.

One of the most fascinating new areas of computer science that has emerged from complexity theory is genetic programming. In this chapter I use this approach to generate a system that uses genetically evolved programs to learn, rather than programs that I created. The Mice in a Maze Lab will be used to explore this concept.

Background of Genetic Programming

Genetic programming relies for its success on the concepts inherent in complexity theory. The fundamental concept is to create a richly interacting system of components that exhibit random behavior. Using some external, evaluative criteria of fitness, those elements that exhibit emergent behavior that is somehow evaluated as good are rewarded by staying alive and being allowed to mate and reproduce. Those elements whose emergent behavior is evaluated as bad are killed off. It's a cold, hard world in the land of genetic programming.

The concept of applying genetic algorithms to computer problems was first developed by John Holland, largely as a result of a graduate class he taught in the 1960s called "Theory of Adaptive Systems." His students successfully applied genetic algorithms to a wide variety of practical problems, including a fascinating program by David Goldberg.

Goldberg was a former pipeline worker studying computer science. He had firsthand experience with the difficulties involved in controlling the flow of a substance (natural gas) through a long pipe.

At periodic intervals along the pipe are independently controllable pumps and pressure gauges. An operator of this system monitors the flow and increases or decreases the pump speeds in an attempt to maintain a constant, optimal pressure throughout the pipeline. Unfortunately, the problem is not as simple as it might appear. Increasing the pump speed to increase pressure at one point may decrease pressure at another point. Periodic oscillations may occur as you attempt to increase pressure but overshoot, then attempt to decrease pressure but undershoot, each time with a greater swing in pressure. Leaks may develop that must be identified, and the operator must avoid attempting to maintain pressure if the decrease in pressure is caused by a leak. In short, the job is difficult at best for a human operator and had never been successfully automated. Using genetic algorithms on an Apple II computer, Goldberg was able to simulate an entire pipeline and successfully control the pumps with genetic algorithms.

REAL WORLD

Actual. Genetic programming holds great promise as an adaptable, highly accurate method of doing pattern recognition. Potential applications include speech recognition, converting printed or handwritten text to digital text, and identifying SCUD missiles from a radar or satellite photograph.

Until recently, biologists largely ignored the concept of computer-based genetic algorithms as an approach to studying genetic behavior and evolution in living systems. One exception was biologist Richard Dawkins. While preparing his book, *The Blind Watchmaker*, Dawkins wrote a computer program on his Macintosh that drew stick figures using random rules. He called these stick figures *biomorphs* and designed the program so that he could select resultant figures that were pleasing to his eye. The program then used genetic algorithms to refine and revise the rules and presented him with a new set of biomorphs from which to select. In surprisingly few generations, the computer was drawing a wide range of plants and insects that were quite recognizable.

Many people have found that genetic algorithms are incredibly effective at a wide variety of game-playing applications. For example, Steven Smith built a genetic program that could play poker. The program quickly beat all earlier programs.

Over time, genetic programming has developed from a cult mentality to a mainstream area of computer science research. The algorithms are extremely robust, responding well to fuzzy or uncertain inputs and extrapolating behavior into new situations with ease. The following sections explain how this is done.

Fundamental Concepts

Genetic programming involves starting with a large number (thousands or tens of thousands are typical) of separate computer programs or rules, each of which is more or less random in its ability to solve a given problem. The programs or rules that are most successful in one generation are kept, mated with each other, occasionally mutated to produce the next generation, and put back into the fray to once again test their ability to solve the problem. This process is called evolution. After thousands of generations, the surviving programs or rules tend to be highly effective at solving the given problem.

All computer programs can be defined in terms of their inputs, processing, and outputs. Genetic programs are no exception. In the case of genetic programs, the processing can be divided into the day-to-day processing by each individual program, and the more global process of evolution. I will address each individually.

Inputs

Genetic programs are normally implemented as rule-based finite state machines. A *state* can be thought of as the machine's current status. For example, you might think of a table lamp as having two states, on and off. A stoplight might have three states: red, yellow, and green. A finite state machine can exist in one or more states and has some way of knowing its current state. A rule-based finite state machine has an internal set of rules that says something like, "If I'm in state A and I get input B, then I should do action C."

For genetic algorithms to work, you need to be able to precisely tell the computer its current state, which can consist of both an internal state that acts as a form of status and the current value for all inputs, which is called the machine's *receptor*. This is normally accomplished by encoding the state and receptor information into a string of digits. These digits can be either binary (0s and 1s) or expressed over some other finite alphabet (for example, A through Z). The values in this string are dictated by the environment and are inputs to the genetic algorithm. They are not part of the genetic algorithm.

The general approach to deriving the input coding for a genetic program is as follows:

1. Define and list the states in which the system can exist.

2. Define the environmental input variables that must be available to the system. The system can solve problems only if the needed data is available to it, so be sure that all needed inputs are present. When you are not sure if an input data item is relevant to the problem at hand or not, include it. The genetic algorithm will make the determination itself and eventually either evolve to use it or to ignore it.

Enter the COMPLEXITY LAB

3. Define the range of possible values for each of the environmental inputs.

4. Map the states and environmental inputs onto a string.

Consider a simple example. Suppose you want to write a genetic program to play Tic-Tac-Toe. The possible states for the program are "It's my turn" or "It's your turn." (We do not need to consider the terminal state of "I've won" or "You've won" because no additional processing occurs at that point.) We might call these two states M for "My turn" and Y for "Your turn."

The environmental input variables consist of a square three-by-three grid, each cell being either blank or containing an *O* or an *X*. Figure 6.1 illustrates a possible matching using a ternary alphabet for the cell values and a binary alphabet for the state values.

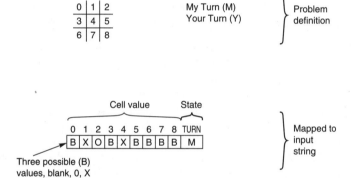

Figure 6.1.
Ternary mapping of the Tic-Tac-Toe problem.

Processing

This section discusses the day-to-day processing that occurs within a single generation. The evolutionary processing that occurs between generations is discussed a bit later in this section.

Processing is accomplished using a series of transition rules. In the Tic-Tac-Toe example, a transition rule might say that, given the input string, BBBBBBBBBM, transition to BBBBXBBBBY. This results in the computer placing an *X* in the center of the board and waiting for the opponent's next move. It is possible to have more than one transition rule for a particular input string. For example, given the same input string, BBBBBBBBBM, another rule must say to change to the output string, XBBBBBBBBY, which results in an *X* being placed in the upper-left corner of the board. An ordinary genetic program simply selects a random rule from those that match. Classifier systems, discussed later in this chapter, use a more sophisticated approach that involves assigning a value to each matching transition rule, causing certain matching rules to be selected more often than other matching rules. Once a particular rule is selected (triggered), it is executed (fired) to produce an output string.

Besides the issue of multiple possible outputs for a single input, genetic algorithms need to deal with the fact that most real-world problems are so complex that it would not be possible to have a unique transition rule for every possible input and system state. Genetic programs solve this problem using wild-card rules. These rules act as defaults, being available for triggering when no more specific rule seems appropriate. Humans use wild-card rules extensively in a wide range of circumstances. For example, "If you can't say something nice, don't say anything at all"; "When in doubt, punt"; or "When playing bridge, lead through strength." Classifier systems represent a wild-card rule using a special symbol—an asterisk (*), for example—to match on anything. For example, the rule, ****B****Y, matches on any Tic-Tac-Toe board configuration that has a blank in the center.

You may wonder where the rules come from. Believe it or not, they're randomly generated. The rules start off completely random; thus the program starts off completely stupid. Over time, programs with a large number of bad rules are weeded out, and programs with good rules remain. In addition, when relatively successful programs "have sex" with each other (as described later in this chapter), they exchange rules to produce "children." In this way, some of their progeny may have an even higher number of the good rules and so be even more likely to survive and reproduce. The number of rules to randomly generate depends on the number of possible input strings. The larger the number of input strings, the more rules that are needed to cover a somewhat reasonable percentage of the possible values. It is amazing, however, that relatively few rules can often handle a wide range of situations.

Another possible approach is to start with only the most general rules. As these general rules are applied, you can keep track of the input string and the eventual outcome, synthesizing more specific rules based on ultimate success or failure. This is probably the approach used by humans when developing rules that govern everyday life.

Another interesting dilemma arises through the use of randomly generated rules. Some of those rules result in an outcome that is illegal by the definition of the problem at hand. In our Tic-Tac-Toe problem, for example,

Enter the COMPLEXITY LAB

nothing stops the computer from generating a rule that would cause it to take two turns in a row. Two alternative approaches can handle this issue of valid versus invalid rules. One possibility is for the programmer to define the criteria that make a rule valid. These are then hard-coded into the program, and any rules that are produced are forced to adhere to the stated criteria. Another approach is to allow invalid rules and then allow the program's opponent (the external environment) to detect the fact that the program is "cheating" and declare that the program lose by default. In effect, you must catch the program cheating, call it a cheat, and shoot it! In this way, rules that result in the program getting caught cheating will be weeded out. Interestingly, when using this approach, rules that cause cheating that the program gets away with are allowed to remain.

Outputs

In a genetic program, some strings that are the result of a particular rule being fired result in an output from the system. In the Tic-Tac-Toe example, each time the program places an X in a new cell, the X can be displayed in the appropriate location on a screen. In the gas pipeline flow control example, outputs might include commands to various pumps controlling their pressure. These outputs are called *effectors* in genetic programming. As with inputs, you need to identify all possible outputs that you expect to come from the program, define the range of possible values for all outputs, then code these outputs onto a string. In some cases, including Tic-Tac-Toe, the inputs and outputs are symmetrical, and the same string coding can be used for both. In the gas pipeline example, the receptor string and effector string coding will be different.

Evolution, Sex, and Mutations

If we just kill off the programs that have a set of ineffective rules and retain and reproduce the programs that have a more effective set of rules, we eventually have a large number of somewhat effective programs. We are limited, however, to the best of the programs randomly generated during the initial period when each program was created. This is probably not a very satisfactory result, because most real applications don't allow us to generate enough individual programs to test more than a tiny percentage of the possible rule combinations. It is for this reason that we use evolutionary processing in genetic programming, and this is where sex and mutation enter the picture.

Sexual Reproduction in Genetic Programming

The basis for the entire theory of genetic programming is biology, in which the DNA strand that contains the genetic blueprint for all creatures is nature's set of rules. In nature, some simple creatures reproduce asexually, but all complex organisms reproduce sexually. Why? It turns out that sexual reproduction, in which the DNA from two partners is combined to form a new DNA strand with characteristics of both parents, results in much faster evolution toward an optimal configuration for the current environment. The children of these sexual unions have various combinations of rules selected from a pool of rules that are known to be good in some sense of the word. Sexual reproduction in genetic programming extends this concept to computer programs.

Recall that rules consist of a finite length input string over some finite alphabet and a matching finite length output string over a possibly different finite alphabet. The genetic programming approach rewards rules that ultimately result in success by allowing them to remain in existence.

When applying sexual reproduction to genetic programs, two approaches can be used either individually or together. After thinning the population down, you can combine traits between survivors on a rule-by-rule basis, where individuals swap entire rules with each other, or you can combine the actual rules, swapping a piece of a successful rule in one survivor with an equal-sized piece of a rule in another survivor. The former approach is primarily used when combined with machine learning, as I'll cover during my discussion of classifier systems later in this chapter. The latter approach is the more traditional and is the primary method in standard genetic programming. The end result of adding sexual reproduction to the genetic program is a greatly improved ability to rapidly adapt to a new environment, with each new generation consisting of combinations of successful traits from the previous generation.

Beware of Mutations

Early researchers in genetic programming hypothesized that mutations, or the random changing of rules, would be an important component of the evolution of these programs. They found, however, that as long as sexual reproduction was present, mutations gave only a very low-order improvement when done very infrequently (about once per thousand changes) and actually hurt matters when done frequently. Nevertheless, mutations play an important role in the genetic algorithms. For a given population, there may be a crucial rule that is absolutely required for survival (or improved performance) that is simply not present in any of the initial rules and cannot

Enter the COMPLEXITY LAB

be synthesized by sexual reproduction of existing rules. Periodic mutations allow the population to carefully explore new rules and test them for effectiveness. Over time, mutated individuals provide new, useful rules that can then be integrated into the population. A stable population can also mutate to adapt to a changing environment.

In the computer, mutations are implemented simply by periodically changing the value of one random position in a rule. Numbers in the range of 1 change per 1,000 bits typically work well. It's hard to imagine a programming concept more foreign to traditional programming than intentionally making random changes to a program's bits!

Complexity Lab

The Complexity Lab, Mice in a Maze, is used to demonstrate various types of genetic programming. I've also designed the application to provide flexibility with respect to how the rules are generated and how the system behaves; this allows you to perform experiments on your own.

Figure 6.2 shows the initial screen for the Mice in a Maze laboratory. The mice start in the lower-left corner of the display and appear to be stacked on top of one another. (The mice quickly move to each of the corners in the display because the mouse world is a toroid.) Their goal, the cheese, is the round circle in the center of the display. The maze is created using a series of randomly positioned black rectangles that act as walls for the mice.

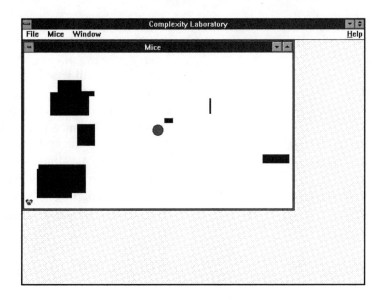

Figure 6.2.
Mice in a Maze.

Figure 6.3 shows the Mice in a Maze Setup dialog box. Table 6.1 describes each of the available fields. For this book, I performed three experiments. In the first, I set the number of rectangles to zero. This enables us to see how well the genetic algorithm works with no obstacles, presumably the simplest case. In the second, I set the number of rectangles to 10. We can thus observe the impact of adding obstacles between the mice and their destination. Finally, I leave the number of rectangles set at 10 and select the Move Cheese check box. This creates the added difficulty of forcing the mice to find a moving target from one generation to the next.

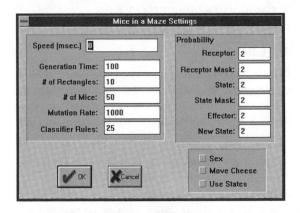

Figure 6.3.
Mice in a Maze
Setup dialog box.

Table 6.1. Mice in a Maze Setup Dialog Box

Field	Default	Meaning
Speed (msec.)	0	Update rate in milliseconds, with 0 being full speed.
Generation Time	100	The number of mice position updates prior to assessing the progress of the mice and creating a new generation.
# of Rectangles	10	The number of randomly generated rectangles that block the mice's progress.
# of Mice	50	The number of mice to create.
Mutation Rate	1000	The mutation rate expressed in mutations per X bits where X defaults to 1000.

Enter the COMPLEXITY LAB

Field	Default	Meaning
Classifier Rules	25	The number of classifier (transition) rules each mouse will have to work with when controlling its behavior.
Receptor Probability	2	For each rule's receptor test, the probability that each individual bit will be set. The receptor test is compared to a receptor input to see if this rule is eligible to be fired. A value of 2 indicates that 1/2 of the bits will be set; a value of 4 means that 1/4 of the bits will be set, and so on.
Receptor Mask	2	This field sets a "don't care" or "wild-card" status for individual receptor bits. A 1 in this field means that all the bits in the receptor mask will be set and will therefore match on any input value. A 2 in this field means that 1/2 of the bits in the mask will be set. A 0 means that none of the bits in the mask will be set and the rules' receptor test must exactly match an input string to be triggered. (A value of 0 generally results in no rules ever being triggered because the default number of rules per mouse is relatively small and the probability that they will exactly match an input string is quite low.)

continues

CHAPTER SIX   **Programming with Genetic Algorithms**

Table 6.1. continued

Field	Default	Meaning
State	2	The probability that individual bits will be set in the transition rule's internal state test field. A value of 2 means that 1/2 of the bits will be set.
State Mask	2	The probability that individual bits will be set in the state mask for the internal state field. This field is similar to the receptor mask field. It allows wild-card status for individual state field bits.
Effector	2	Probability that each bit in the Effector output for this rule will be set, with 2 indicating a probability of 50 percent.
New State	2	Probability that each bit in the new internal state output for this rule will be set to 1.

In all cases, I check the Sex check box and do not check the Use States check box. Leaving the Sex check box unchecked results in much slower learning. Checking the Use States check box allows the mice to use an internal state field when deciding whether a rule should be available for use.

The Implementation of Mice in a Maze

The receptor for the Mice in a Maze problem consists of sixteen bits. The first eight bits correspond to the locations that are North, Northeast, East, Southeast, South, Southwest, West, and Northwest from the current location. If a bit is set, it indicates that the corresponding direction is blocked by a rectangle. The second eight bits also correspond to the locations that are North, Northeast, East, Southeast, South, Southwest, West, and Northwest from the current location, but in this case three bits are set in the general direction of the cheese. For example, if the cheese is due west of the mouse, the West, Northwest, and Southwest bits all would be set. (These bits can be considered receptor hints that correspond to the "smell" of the cheese.)

The internal state field consists of three bits whose meaning is not defined. States are sometimes useful for a genetic program to keep track of something internally. They act as a genetic program's memory. For example, when running a maze it might be handy to have a state field that tells you the current direction you are traveling or that indicates whether you turned right or left last time. The use of memory must evolve just as the use of rules evolves. Mice who use memory well (or have good memory) should have a survival advantage over mice who don't use memory well. It would be an interesting experiment to explore whether the state field improves the performance of the mice in running the maze. The number and length of experiments required to test this theory exceeds the scope of this book. However, I have included the Use State check box in the mice setup dialog box so that you can run experiments with "mouse memory" on your own.

The Effector field, used for the output from the rule, consists of eight bits that tell the mouse whether it should move North, Northeast, East, Southeast, South, Southwest, West, or Northwest.

The rules initially consist of a completely random receptor field, receptor mask, state field, state mask, effector field, and new state field. We therefore expect the mice to initially move in random directions. If a mouse tries to move through a wall, it is not allowed to move at all. When a mouse reaches the cheese, it is held at that position (imagine that it becomes too busy eating to think about running around any more).

If more than one rule is eligible for firing, one of the eligible rules is selected randomly. If no rule is eligible for firing, the mouse is moved in a random direction.

Mouse reproduction involves keeping the top 10 percent (those mice closest to the cheese) and mating them with each other. Mating involves swapping individual rule field values (including masks) at random locations. During mating, the new mice take on the colors of the top 10 percent. You will notice as you run experiments that successful mice soon dominate the color scheme of the population. (When sex is not turned on, the top 10 percent are cloned to produce the next generation.)

Mice in a Maze, No Obstacles, Fixed Cheese

Before we begin the experiments it is important for you to keep in mind that each run of an experiment will be unique. As a result, you should expect the results that appear on your computer screen to differ slightly from the results presented in the following sections. In addition, you may notice that after a few generations, when mouse movement becomes less random, many mice will occupy the same position on the display. It will appear as though there are only 2 or 3 mice on the screen. As soon as one reaches the cheese, however, the status message, `"Mice at Cheese"`, will increment by the number of mice occupying that screen position.

Our initial experiment uses the simplest case. We have no rectangles, mice sex is set to on, and the cheese does not move. Figure 6.4 shows the proper values in the Setup dialog box, and Figure 6.5 shows the resultant starting position with the Mice in a Maze window maximized.

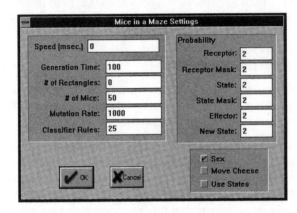

Figure 6.4.
Initial experiment setup dialog values.

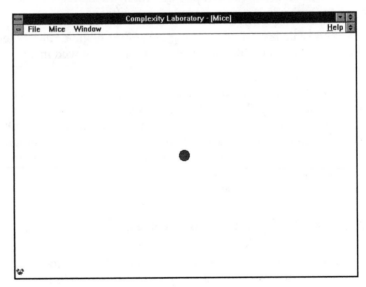

Figure 6.5.
Initial display of Mice in a Maze for the first experiment.

Figure 6.6 shows the display after 98 mouse moves. As you can see, only one mouse has successfully managed to find the cheese. Overall, the mice seem to be more or less randomly distributed over the display.

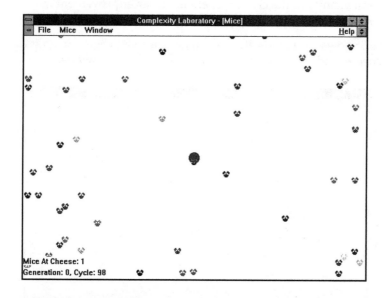

Figure 6.6.
Mice in a Maze, first experiment, first generation.

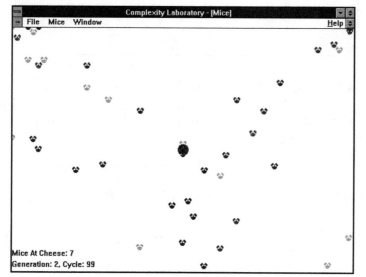

Figure 6.7.
Mice in a Maze, first experiment, second generation.

Figure 6.7 shows the continuation of the first experiment, this time after 2 generations and 99 moves into the third generation. At this point, 7 mice have found the cheese, and the remaining mice are beginning to converge in the general vicinity of the cheese. There is a clear improvement in performance over the first run within a mere 2 generations.

Figure 6.8 shows the results after seven generations. There are now 12 mice at the cheese, and the movement toward the cheese is obvious.

Figure 6.8.
Mice in a Maze, first experiment, seventh generation.

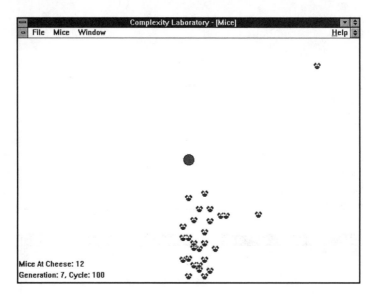

Mice in a Maze, Obstacles, Fixed Cheese

Figure 6.9 shows the Setup dialog box properly configured for the second experiment. In this experiment we introduce 10 randomly positioned rectangles onto the maze as obstacles.

Figure 6.10 shows the results of the second experiment on the first generation after 99 mouse movements. Once again, one mouse has found the cheese and the remainder are relatively randomly distributed.

Enter the COMPLEXITY LAB

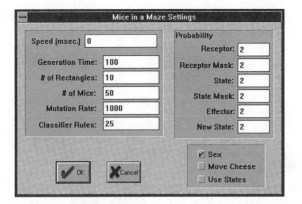

Figure 6.9.
*Mice in a Maze,
second experiment
Setup dialog box.*

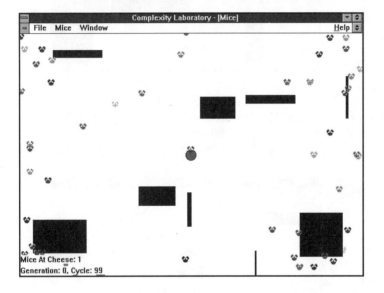

Figure 6.10.
*Mice in a Maze,
second experiment,
first generation.*

Figure 6.11 shows the results after three generations and 99 mouse movements. Eight mice have found the cheese in spite of the rectangles, and the movement toward the cheese is obvious.

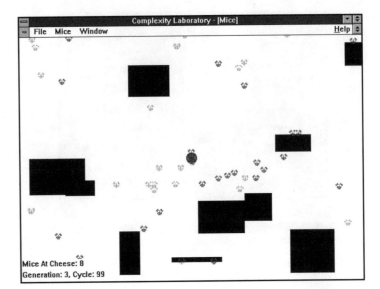

Figure 6.11.
*Mice in a Maze,
second experiment,
third generation.*

Figure 6.12 shows the results after eight generations and 99 mouse movements. An impressive 45 mice have found the cheese, and the remaining mice are nearly there. This population obviously started out with some very effective maze-running rules created by the random generation process.

Figure 6.12.
*Mice in a Maze,
second experiment,
eighth generation.*

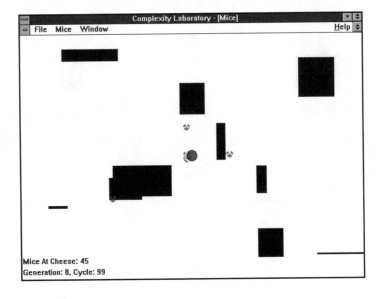

Enter the COMPLEXITY LAB

Mice in a Maze, Obstacles, Random Cheese

It might be tempting to think that the mice simply move to the middle of the screen and ignore receptor hints corresponding to the smell of the cheese. This can be tested by putting the cheese at a random location for each run, which can be accomplished by checking the Move Cheese check box. Figure 6.13 shows the setup dialog box settings for the third Mice in a Maze experiment.

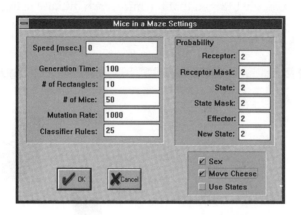

Figure 6.13.
*Mice in a Maze,
third experiment
Setup dialog box.*

Figure 6.14 shows the results for the first generation after 99 mouse movements. No mice have found the cheese, and the mice are relatively randomly positioned.

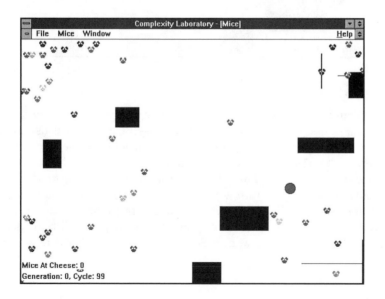

Figure 6.14.
*Mice in a Maze,
third experiment,
first generation.*

CHAPTER SIX   **Programming with Genetic Algorithms**

Figure 6.15 shows the results after 2 generations and 99 mouse movements. Four mice have found the cheese, and a slight tendency to move toward the cheese can be observed.

Finally, Figure 6.16 shows the results after 5 generations and 99 mouse movements. Seventeen mice have found the cheese and the movement toward the cheese is obvious. It is clear, even with randomly positioned obstacles and a moving target, that the mice, each initially using a completely random set of rules, are able to evolve to effectively solve the problem of finding the cheese.

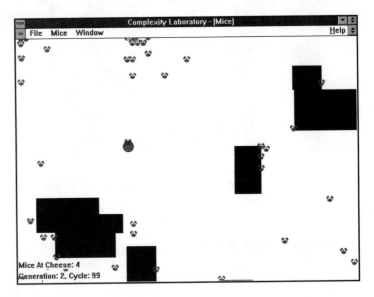

Figure 6.15.
Mice in a Maze,
third experiment,
second generation.

Specialization

One problem faced by both nature and genetic programs is where a trait is useful for a period of time, then stops being useful, and later is useful again. For example, suppose a chess program has a particularly useful response to a given play that results in a win every time. Now suppose the opponent recognizes this defense and avoids that situation for a long period of time. Eventually, the chess program will not consider this rule especially valuable because it is never used. It may even be purged from the population as a useless rule. Now suppose a new opponent tries the play. With the defense rule gone, the population is at risk. Solving this problem is the topic of this section.

Enter the COMPLEXITY LAB

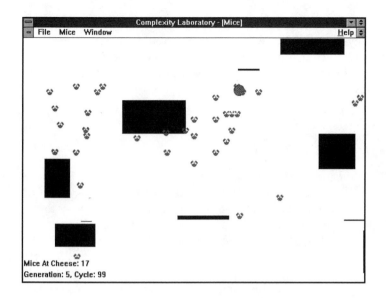

Figure 6.16.
*Mice in a Maze,
third experiment,
fifth generation.*

Shielding Characteristics with Recessive Traits

One early problem with genetic algorithms was overspecialization and temporally specialized solutions. The systems were sufficiently chaotic that they found optimal solutions for the moment, discarding lessons learned from the past that were temporarily not useful. Nature has developed an intricate system to avoid this problem: recessive genes. Applying this concept to computer-based genetic algorithms is one of the newest areas of computer science research.

The Model in Nature

In nature, many genetic characteristics are either dominant or recessive. For example, blue eyes are a recessive gene, while brown eyes are dominant. A gene pair is used to control the actual eye color. Suppose that we represent a blue eye tendency with a lowercase *b* and a brown eye tendency with an uppercase *B*. In biology, it is traditional to represent recessive genes with lowercase letters and dominant genes with uppercase letters. Let's start with a blue-eyed individual (*bb*) mating with a pure brown-eyed individual (*BB*). Their children will all be mixed (*Bb* or *bB*). Because *B* is dominant, they will all have brown eyes. Now suppose two mixed individuals mate with each other. The possible combinations are: *bb*, *bB*, *Bb*, and *BB*. One-quarter of their children will have blue eyes, and the remainder will have brown eyes. Now let's suppose that a blue-eyed individual mates with a mixed individual. The blue-eyed individual will always contribute a *b* gene. The mixed individual will contribute either a *b* or a *B* gene. One-half of their children will have blue eyes and one-half will have brown eyes and be mixed genetically.

REAL WORLD

Actual. One big advantage of genetic programming is its ability to help scientists better understand how human genes work. Computer scientists observing real life gain valuable lessons that improve their computer models, and biologists observing computer models gain a better understanding of real life.

Why has nature evolved this complicated structure of recessive and dominant genetic traits? It appears that in many cases, the recessive trait may be a characteristic that was useful to survival at some point in the past but that is no longer useful. Because it is recessive, the trait is not predominant in the population, but because it is shielded by the more useful dominant trait, it is able to remain in the gene pool. If conditions change in the future so that the once-useful trait is again needed, it can be found hiding behind the dominant shield. This theory is backed up in part by the fact that the dominant/recessive relationship of genes can, and does, change with changes in the environment. One classic example is a small moth that lives in England. The moth can be either light or dark in color, based on a gene pair. The light color was initially dominant, and the light-colored moths were successfully camouflaged from competitors against light-colored tree bark and rocks. The industrial revolution in England resulted in a lot of sooty surfaces in the cities, making the light-colored moth an obvious victim. The dark gene then became dominant because the moths that tended to be dark were able to successfully hide against sooty surfaces. Finally, as the air has become cleaner and surfaces have lightened, the white gene is once again becoming dominant.

Enter the COMPLEXITY LAB

REAL WORLD

Potential. One potential use of genetic programs is to analyze brain waves of people in comas. By monitoring the brain waves of a large number of patients and being told which patients came out of comas and when, the genetic programs may eventually evolve to the point where they can predict which patients will emerge and perhaps give an indication of when the coma will end.

Implementing Recessive Traits in a Computer

Recessive traits can be implemented in computers in a manner very similar to nature, and they may achieve a similar benefit. For all rules where we wish to maintain a dominant-recessive relationship, we must maintain two copies of each rule in each organism and tag each copy with a field that indicates whether the rule is dominant (D) or recessive (d). The initialization of these fields can be random. When selecting a rule, we look to the rule pair and use the dominant rule. If there are two dominant or two recessive rules, we randomly pick one.

During sexual reproduction, we select a random rule from the rule pairs of both parents and combine them into the offspring. The dominant or recessive characteristic of each rule follows it to the offspring.

To simulate nature's ability to make a dominant gene recessive (and vice versa) as a survival skill, during each generation we select a small percentage of the population and change the dominance relationship for one of its rules. In other words, for a given rule pair we make the recessive rule dominant and the dominant rule recessive. If the time is ripe for this recessive trait to reemerge, this individual will survive and flourish, thus passing the new dominance relationship into the gene pool.

Object-Oriented Genetics

One difficulty that continuously arises in genetic programming is the fact that many rules cannot simply be randomly spliced together. In DNA, the location of the rule (gene) on the strand determines the function (whether it is a gene for eye color or hair color), and the specific chemicals present at that location determine the nature of the gene's characteristic (if the gene is for eye color, whether that color is blue or brown). For example, the gene that controls blue or brown eyes is always found in the same location on the DNA strand. During sexual reproduction, you get either a blue eye gene or a brown eye gene, not some combination of the two that has no meaning.

REAL WORLD

Potential. Many factors go into determining whether a specific operation will do more harm than good for a significant number of elderly patients. It is possible that a genetic program can evolve the expertise to take as input a wide range of factors about the patient and the operation, then determine whether the operation is worth the risk or not.

Using object-oriented programming techniques, it may be possible to encode various genetic traits (expressed as behavioral traits in most computer programs) as C++ classes that can take on specific values and have specific characteristics. The program's "DNA strand" could then consist of an array or similar structure containing pointers to the appropriate genes (classes). During sexual reproduction, the parental arrays could be swapped at an arbitrary location when creating the child without being afraid of splitting a gene. If dominant and recessive traits are used, the individual C++ classes could be used to store and work out dominant relationships. This is an area with potential, but one which I have not seen explored.

Red Queen Learning

By their very nature, genetic programs are continuously learning. As you present the program with new challenges, it will adapt to the new environment and improve its performance. One difficulty with this approach, however, is that the genetic program only becomes as good as necessary to succeed in the given environment. For example, suppose you wrote a genetic program to play chess and then played games of chess with the program over and over. Initially, you would have little difficulty defeating it. Over time, the games would become more and more challenging. Eventually, you would find yourself in a situation where the genetic program could consistently beat you. At this point, the genetic program stops improving its playing ability. If a chess player came along who was better than you, that player would not find the program challenging. More significantly, if the program were never given new opponents, it would be prevented from exploring new heights of mastery because of the limitations in its single opponent. One solution to this limitation is a concept called *red queen learning*, which is discussed in the following sections.

The Treadmill

In Lewis Carroll's book, *Alice in Wonderland*, there is a scene in which Alice is running alongside the red queen but they are not getting anywhere. Alice asks why they do not seem to be moving, and the red queen replies that in Wonderland people need to run faster and faster just to stay in the same place. Red queen learning, named for this scene, is a form of competitive learning in which both the proponent (our genetic program) and the opponent are continuously improving. This is typically implemented using two learning systems competing against each other. For example, two genetic programs may compete in chess with each other. The end result is a spiral of continuous improvements as both programs become better and better. This form of learning often results in explorations of sophisticated and surprising strategies for achieving success.

Nature uses red queen learning extensively in its evolutionary model. The wolves get stronger, the rabbits get faster, the wolves get better at stalking, the rabbits get better at hiding, and so on. Mankind has presented many unique challenges to nature's creatures, and many of them are learning to overcome these challenges through evolution and red queen learning. Two somewhat scary examples are the ever-increasing resistance of insects to the ever-increasing toxicity of insecticides and the ever-increasing resistance of bacteria to the ever-increasing potency of antibiotics.

One early example of red queen learning applied to genetic programming was a classic program called Echo.

An Artificial Ecology

Echo, which is short for ecosystem, was first developed by John Holland. Echo is an artificial environment consisting of a flat plain with scattered ponds that contain nutrients. Holland's organisms moved around this plain, eating nutrients whenever they came across them. When one organism met another, they engaged in a form of computer hand-to-hand combat. The two organisms' chromosomes (represented by a string) were compared to determine which organism was more fit. The survivor ate the loser by taking on all of its internal resources. If it then had enough internal resources to reproduce, it made a copy of itself with an occasional mutation thrown in for good luck. It then went back to grazing. When running Echo, Holland discovered a very realistic phenomenon in which the organisms slowly evolved (through mutation) ever more powerful offensive and defensive capabilities.

Echo was somewhat unique, not just in its implementation of red queen learning but also because it used a different form of genetic programming called *machine learning*. In traditional genetic programming, the organisms themselves (complete with their entire suite of rules) reproduce or are killed off. Genetic-based machine learning, on the other hand, allows an individual organism to learn and adapt while remaining alive. This is accomplished by assigning a value weight to individual rules within the organism's reper- toire of rules, and using a form of sexual reproduction between successful rules within the organism. Systems that use this form of genetic-based machine learning are called *classifier systems*.

Classifier systems give each rule a value weight. The value weight is some- thing that changes with time; successful rules go up in value, while rules that fail go down in value. The value weight is used to select between *candidate rules* (the rules that are eligible for activation based on the current receptor and internal state). Original efforts in this area unearthed a com- mon difficulty in which rules with lower value ratings were never fired and hence did not have the opportunity to improve their value weight. A solution that is almost universal in classifier systems is to use a probabilistic approach to selecting rules. You can think of it as a computerized lottery, with all eligible rules holding one or more tickets. The rules with a high value weight hold lots of tickets, while the rules with low value weights hold just a few, but anybody can win.

Assigning and changing the value ratings for the rules is an art in itself. The problem is, which rules do you reward, and when? Continuing with the earlier Tic-Tac-Toe example, it is obvious that the rules that put the winning

X in a square should be rewarded with a higher value weight, but what about the rules that allowed the game to evolve to the state where the winning X could be put on the board? They need to be rewarded too, but when they are activated, the system has no way of knowing whether they will ultimately result in a winning game or a losing game. John Holland solved the problem rather elegantly using an approach called the *bucket brigade*.

Rules start off equal. When the first rule is triggered, its value weight is decreased as a form of payment for the right to be activated. When the second rule is triggered, its value weight is decreased, and the payment is given to the first rule, thus increasing the first rule's strength. Ultimately, the final rules that result in a win (or other externally determined situation involving a reward) are rewarded from the external environment and the chain is completed. Final rules that result in a loss (or other externally determined situation involving a punishment) are not rewarded from the external environment and hence remain weakened and less likely to be activated in the future. Because rewards are effectively passed from the external environment to a long chain of rules that result in the reward being given, this algorithm is called the bucket brigade.

The classifier system approach is an excellent example of machine learning. Almost invariably, it is also an example of emergent behavior, because a relatively few rules result in surprising, complex behavior. The optimization of rule weights using the bucket brigade algorithm will find the best possible configuration from the original pool of rules generated randomly. With the addition of sexual reproduction and mutation, classifier systems evolve in much the same way as the more traditional genetic programming example described earlier in this chapter.

Applications of Genetic Programming

REAL WORLD

Potential. Genetic programming may hold promise for a wide range of expert systems in which the rules are not clearly understood. Examples might include medical diagnosis, predicting energy usage in a city, and predicting the number of claims an insurance carrier will be faced with in a given month.

Genetic programming techniques should be considered in any situation in which the input data and desired outputs can be coded over a finite alphabet; the relationship between the input data and the output data is not well understood; outputs are not required to be exactly right 100 percent of the time, but must be reasonable given inaccuracies or unusual changes in the input data; there is no requirement that the programmer or analyst be able to explain in detail exactly why a specified conclusion was reached; and sufficient historical data (or an available opponent, in the case of a game application) allows the genetic algorithms to learn and evolve. Applications that meet these criteria abound, including stock market analysis, medical diagnosis, pattern recognition, and delivery routing. It also seems likely that future programs that more closely approximate human thinking will probably use some variation of genetic programming, learning how to think in the same way a human child learns to think rather than being taught how to think by a programmer.

Enter the COMPLEXITY LAB

For Programmers Only

The Mice in a Maze program is one of the most complicated in the Complexity Lab. It required four classes that are unique to this lab. The WMiceDialog class handles the Setup dialog box. WMouseWindow implements the main window and controls all of the overall processing. Each mouse is encapsulated in a class called WMice. Within each mouse, the individual rules are encapsulated in a class called WMouseRule.

The MouseDialog structure, shown below, is used as a transfer buffer to communicate with the WMiceDialog class.

```
struct MiceTransfer
{
    char Rate [6];
    char GenerationTime [8];
    char Rectangles [8];
    char TotalMice [8];
    char Mutation [8];
    char Classifier [8];
    char Receptor [6];
    char ReceptorMask [6];
    char State [6];
    char StateMask [6];
    char Effector [6];
    char NewState [6];
    BOOL MiceSex;
    BOOL MoveCheese;
    BOOL UseState;

    MiceTransfer()
    {
        strcpy (Rate, "0");
        strcpy (GenerationTime, "100");
        strcpy (Rectangles, "10");
        strcpy (TotalMice, "50");
        strcpy (Mutation, "1000");
        strcpy (Classifier, "25");
        strcpy (Receptor, "2");
        strcpy (ReceptorMask, "2");
        strcpy (State, "2");
        strcpy (StateMask, "2");
        strcpy (Effector, "2");
        strcpy (NewState, "2");
        MiceSex = FALSE;
        MoveCheese = FALSE;
        UseState = FALSE;
    };
};
```

WMiceDialog Class Design

Figure 6.17 shows the class design for the WMiceDialog class, and Table 6.2 describes the member function.

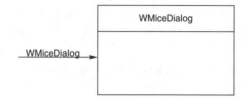

Figure 6.17.
WMiceDialog class design.

```
WMiceDialog(PTWindowsObject Parent,
            struct MiceTransfer*);
```

Table 6.2. WMiceDialog Member Function Descriptions

Member Function	Description
WMiceDialog	Constructor

WMiceWindow Class Design

Figure 6.18 illustrates the class design for the WMiceWindow class, and Table 6.3 describes each of the member functions for the class.

Enter the COMPLEXITY LAB

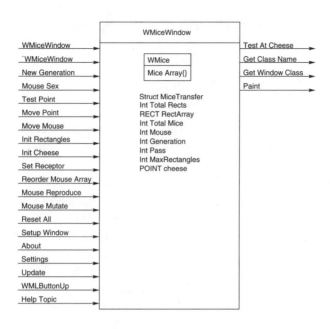

WMiceWindow		
WMiceWindow		Test At Cheese
`WMiceWindow		Get Class Name
New Generation		Get Window Class
Mouse Sex	WMice	Paint
Test Point	Mice Array{}	
Move Point		
Move Mouse	Struct MiceTransfer	
Init Rectangles	Int Total Rects	
Init Cheese	RECT RectArray	
Set Receptor	Int Total Mice	
Reorder Mouse Array	Int Mouse	
Mouse Reproduce	Int Generation	
Mouse Mutate	Int Pass	
Reset All	Int MaxRectangles	
Setup Window	POINT cheese	
About		
Settings		
Update		
WMLButtonUp		
Help Topic		

Figure 6.18.
WMiceWindow class design.

```
       void NewGeneration();
       void MouseSex();
       BOOL TestPoint(POINT);
       void MovePoint(POINT&,int X,int Y);
       void MoveMouse();
       void InitRectangles();
       void InitCheese();
       void SetReceptor(POINT &P, WBit &Receptor);
       void MoveMouse(POINT &P, WBit &Effector);
       void ReorderMouseArray ();
       void MouseReproduce();
       void MouseMutate ();
       BOOL TestAtCheese(POINT &P);

       WMiceWindow(PTWindowsObject Frame);
       ~WMiceWindow();

       void ResetAll();

       void SetupWindow();
       LPSTR GetClassName ();
       void GetWindowsClass (WNDCLASS &);
       void Paint (HDC PaintDC, PAINTSTRUCT& ps);

       void About (RTMessage)=
              [CM_FIRST+CM_About];
       void Settings (RTMessage)=
              [CM_FIRST+CM_Setup];
       void Update (RTMessage)=
              [WM_FIRST+WM_TIMER];
       void WMLButtonUp (RTMessage)=
              [WM_FIRST+WM_LBUTTONUP];
       void Help Topic ()=[CM_FIRST+CM_HelpTopic];
```

Table 6.3. `WMiceWindow` **Member Function Descriptions**

Member Function	Description
WMiceWindow	Constructor.
~WMiceWindow	Destructor.
NewGeneration	Performs all processing necessary when a new generation of mice must be created.
MouseSex	Implements sex between two mice.
TestPoint	Tests to see if a given point is inside any of the rectangles.
MovePoint	Moves a point in the specified direction up to 10 pixels away, or until a rectangle is encountered.
MoveMouse	Moves a mouse in the direction indicated by its currently active effector.
InitRectangles	Initializes the rectangles to random positions.
InitCheese	Initializes the cheese position.
SetReceptor	Sets the receptor value for a given mouse based on the relative position of the cheese and the proximity of rectangles.
ReorderMouseArray	Reorders the mice with the ones closest to the cheese at the beginning of the array.
MouseReproduce	Replaces the bottom 90 percent of the mice with new mice that result from the reproduction of the top 10 percent.

Enter the COMPLEXITY LAB

Member Function	Description
MouseMutate	Mutates a mouse.
ResetAll	Resets all variables to their default values.
SetupWindow	Initializes the window.
About	Displays the Mice in a Maze About dialog box.
Settings	Displays the Mice in a Maze Setup dialog box.
Update	Updates the positions of some of the mice, with the exact number being based on the CPU speed.
WMLButtonUp	Adds a user-marked rectangle to the mice maze.
HelpTopic	Displays help on the Mice in a Maze lab.
TestAtCheese	Returns true if a given point is within the boundary of the cheese.
GetClassName	Returns "WMiceWindow".
GetWindowClass	Sets the icon for this window.
Paint	Draws the mice and rectangles.

WMice Class Design

Figure 6.19 illustrates the design of the WMice class, and Table 6.4 describes each of the member functions for the class.

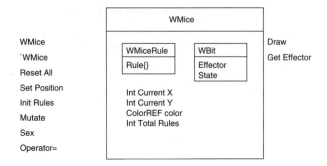

Figure 6.19.
WMice class design.

```
WMice();
virtual~WMice();

virtual void ResetAll(void);

void Draw(HDC);
void SetPosition(int X,int Y);
void InitRules(int Number,
                           int ReceptorProb,
                           int ReceptorMaskProb,
                           int StateProb,
                           int StateMaskProb,
                           int EffectorProb,
                           int NewStateProb);
RWBit GetEffector (RWBit Receptor, BOOL UseState);
void Mutate(int Rate);
void Sex(PWMice);

WMice& operator=(RWMice);
WMice& operator=(PWMice);
```

Table 6.4. WMice Member Function Descriptions

Member Function	Description
WMice	Constructor.
~WMice	Destructor.
ResetAll	Resets all variables to their default values.

Enter the COMPLEXITY LAB

Member Function	Description
SetPosition	Sets the mouse position to a new X and Y value.
InitRules	Initializes each of the rules in the array.
Mutate	Mutates each rule in the array.
Sex	Have sex with another mouse.
operator =	Assigns one WMice object to another.
Draw	Draws this mouse in the mouse's color with the exclusive OR pen. Using the exclusive OR pen allows the mouse to be erased by drawing it again in the same location.
GetEffector	Gets the effector value for a random valid rule given a receptor and current state.

WMouseRule Class Design

Figure 6.20 illustrates the design of the WMouseRule class, and Table 6.5 describes each of the class member functions.

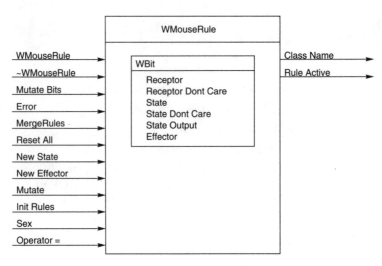

Figure 6.20.
WMouseRule class design.

```
void MutateBits(RWBit,int Odds);
void Error(char*Output);
void MergeRules(RWBit,RWBit);

WMouseRule();
virtual~WMouseRule();

virtual void ResetAll(void);
virtual WStr ClassName();

BOOL RuleActive(RWBit NewReceptor,RWBit NewState);
BOOL RuleActive(RWBit NewReceptor);
RWBit NewState();
RWBit NewEffector();
void Mutate(int);
void InitRules(
                              int ReceptorProb,
                              int ReceptorMaskProb,
                              int StateProb,
                              int StateMaskProb,
                              int EffectorProb,
                              int NewStateProb);
void Sex(PWMouseRule);
WMouseRule& operator=(RWMouseRule);
WMouseRule& operator=(PWMouseRule);
```

Enter the COMPLEXITY LAB

Table 6.5. `WMouseRule` **Member Function Descriptions**

Member Function	Description
`WMouseRule`	Constructor.
`~WMouseRule`	Destructor.
`MutateBits`	Mutates the bits in a single one of the bit arrays in the rule.
`Error`	Displays an error message if an invalid receptor or internal state is passed in.
`MergeRules`	Merges two bit arrays, a subset of sex for the entire rule.
`ResetAll`	Resets all variables to their default values.
`NewState`	Returns the new state dictated by this rule.
`NewEffector`	Returns the effector dictated by this rule.
`Mutate`	Mutates all of the bit arrays in this rule.
`InitRules`	Initializes all bit arrays in this rule.
`Sex`	Implements sex for each of the bit arrays in this rule.
`operator =`	Assigns one `WMouseRule` to another.
`ClassName`	Returns `"WMouseRule"`.
`RuleActive`	Returns true if this rule is valid for the given receptor (and optionally, internal state).

Chapter

7

Concluding
NOTES

A sampling of areas where complexity may be useful.

In this book I've given you a whirlwind tour of many aspects of the emerging science of complexity. Seldom is a new area for scientific study discovered, much less one with the potential to answer so many of nature's fundamental questions. This field has almost unlimited potential to provide new insights into virtually every branch of science. The following come to mind.

Computer Science

The genetic programming algorithms that have come out of this field are among the most powerful, if not *the* most powerful, techniques for developing a wide range of applications, including those in the areas of modeling and simulation, image and pattern recognition, and expert systems. The distributed approach to building the intelligence for a system as a set of interacting modules, each with local knowledge and decisions, will revolutionize many aspects of robotics, factory automation, and similar computer-controlled devices. Looking further into the future, the theories of complexity seem to offer the first real hope of eventually building a computer with something approaching human-like behavior and intelligence.

Biology

Complexity theory has already begun to open the doors on many mysteries of genetics and evolution. It is now becoming clear that interactions and relationships between the various parts of the DNA strand are as important as the individual amino acids that make up the DNA strand. Activities that seem to simulate cell differentiation in a relatively simple computer program (for example, L-Systems) with purely local rules of behavior may explain how cell differentiation works in higher organisms, including humans. Group behaviors, such as those exhibited by social insects (for example, ants) and pack species (for example, birds and fish) may be understood by identifying localized, plausible rules that can be implemented on a computer and which result in the same behavior as that observed in nature. Even something as fundamental as the origin of life may be explained by something predicted by complexity theory, *autocatalytic sets*.

An autocatalytic set is a chain of catalytic reactions that ultimately turns back onto itself. For example, suppose molecule A helps in the formation of molecule B, which helps in the formation of molecule C, which helps in the formation of molecule A. The more A there is, the more B is produced. The more B there is, the more C is produced. The more C there is, the more A is produced, and the chain continues. Computer simulations of the initial primordial soup that existed prior to life forming on earth indicate that an autocatalytic cycle such as this, was not just possible, but almost inevitable. It appears possible that the creation of life was not so much a miraculous event to be marveled at, but the natural and inevitable consequence of a system containing the necessary ingredients needed for an autocatalytic reaction to begin.

Ecology

Ecological systems, by their very nature, are interacting systems operating at the threshold of stability and chaos. Their behaviors are incredibly complex and often cannot be predicted or explained by any other means than computer modeling based on the principles of complexity.

Physics

Traditional physics attempted to break a problem down into individual components and then study those components. In some cases, this is probably appropriate. A large number of physical phenomena, however, is driven, not by the individual actions of components, but by the interactions of the pieces within the context of the system. Examples are found in such diverse areas as particle physics and black holes. The principles of complexity theory open a new avenue to exploring these topics.

Medicine

Perhaps no better example of a complex system exists than the human body and the mind itself. In many ways, we seem to understand more about the origin and operation of the universe than we do about the origin and operation of ourselves. Perhaps looking at the mind as a complex network, in which the interactions between neurons *are* the thought and memories rather than merely a method of communicating, will provide us with new answers and insights. Over time, perhaps some of the complex interactions within the body can be better understood and dealt with through appropriate modeling. Examples of this being applied might include the ability to better predict whether an operation will save a life or cost one, whether the immune system will fight off an infection on its own or will fail, and whether a person will come out of a coma.

Appendix

A

Tailoring the

Complexity

LABS

*Personalizing
the programs on the
accompanying
disk*

As you experiment with the various complexity laboratories, you may find yourself wanting to go beyond the flexibility I built into the lab. I encourage you to use the provided labs as a framework for building your own experiments that push the frontier of our knowledge about complexity. This chapter provides some basic guidelines for tailoring the labs to suit your own needs and desires. I assume that you have a basic understanding of C++ and the Borland C++ compiler with its application framework tools (for example, the Resource Workshop). If you need a basic introduction to C++, you may want to read my book, *Programming Windows with Borland C++* (Ziff-Davis). For a more advanced treatment of this topic, I refer you to my book, *Uncharted Windows Programming* (Sams Publishing). If you've read some books on C++ but don't quite have the hang of it yet, tailoring this existing code might just be the first step you need to become comfortable with this highly popular language.

The Complexity Lab was implemented in Version 3.1 of the Borland C++ compiler. Before you begin tailoring the Complexity Lab, it would be a good idea to verify that you are able to rebuild the Complexity Lab from the source code. This source code is included on the Complexity Lab installation disk and should be installed in the directory c:\complex\source. Using Borland's Open Project command from the Project menu, open the Complex.prj file and verify the locations (path names) of all the files listed in the project's window. If the location of a file is incorrect, make a note of the filename and use the Delete Item command from the Project menu to delete the file from the project. Use the Insert Item command from the Project menu to reinsert the file with the correct path name. (Pay special attention to the Owl.def file. This file should be located in the c:\borlandc\owl\lib directory.) After you verify the locations of the project's files, you can rebuild the project using the Build All command from the Compile menu. You will need approximately 4M of free space on your hard disk to rebuild the project.

Tailoring the Attractors Lab

I've provided you with code that supports two basic equations for attractors, the Lorenz equation and the Julian equation. For these two equations, I provide quite a bit of flexibility—but what if you want to try your own equation? You can make the change easily using the approach described in this section.

Enter the COMPLEXITY LAB

Modifying the Setup Dialog Resource

You probably want to modify the Setup dialog box to include a radio button that will enable you to select your custom equation for processing. This involves four steps. First, you must create a new identifier for your radio button in the DCOMPLEX.H file. For example, you might want to add the line

```
#define IDD_CustomEquation 1001
```

Second, you need to use the dialog editor in the Resource Workshop to increase the size of the existing radio button group box and to add a new radio button with the identifier IDD_CustomEquation (or whatever name you selected for your new identifier). Figure A.1 illustrates this process.

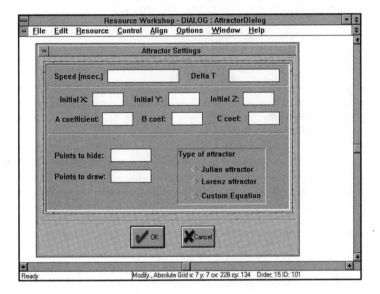

Figure A.1.
Adding a new radio button to the Attractor Setup dialog.

Third, you need to modify the AttractorTransfer transfer buffer structure to include an element corresponding to your new dialog box. This code is found in the WATTRDIA.H file. The following code fragment shows the transfer buffer after this change:

```
struct AttractorTransfer
{
    char Rate [6];
    char InitialX [MAX_NUMERIC];
    char InitialY [MAX_NUMERIC];
    char InitialZ [MAX_NUMERIC];
    char ACoefficient [MAX_NUMERIC];
```

```
        char BCoefficient [MAX_NUMERIC];
        char CCoefficient [MAX_NUMERIC];
        char DeltaTime [MAX_NUMERIC];
        char PointsToHide [MAX_NUMERIC];
        char PointsToDraw [MAX_NUMERIC];
        WORD JulianAttractor;
        WORD LorenzAttractor;
        WORD CustomAttractor; // Added code here!!!!

        AttractorTransfer ()
        {
            strcpy (Rate, "0");
            strcpy (InitialX, "0");
            strcpy (InitialY, "1");
            strcpy (InitialZ, "0");
            strcpy (ACoefficient, ".2");
            strcpy (BCoefficient, ".2");
            strcpy (CCoefficient, "5.7");
            strcpy (DeltaTime, ".04");
            strcpy (PointsToHide, "500");
            strcpy (PointsToDraw, "10000");
            JulianAttractor = TRUE;
            LorenzAttractor = FALSE;
            CustomAttractor=FALSE; // Added code here!!!!
        };
    };
```

Finally, add a line of code to the WAttractorDialog class to actually create
your new radio button object. The following code fragment illustrates this
addition:

```
WAttractorDialog::WAttractorDialog (PTWindowsObject Parent,
    struct AttractorTransfer *tb)
    : TDialog (Parent, "AttractorDialog")
{
    PTGroupBox AttractorGroup;

    new TEdit (this, IDD_Rate, 6);
    new TEdit (this, IDD_InitialX, MAX_NUMERIC);
    new TEdit (this, IDD_InitialY, MAX_NUMERIC);
    new TEdit (this, IDD_InitialZ, MAX_NUMERIC);
    new TEdit (this, IDD_ACoefficient, MAX_NUMERIC);
    new TEdit (this, IDD_BCoefficient, MAX_NUMERIC);
    new TEdit (this, IDD_CCoefficient, MAX_NUMERIC);
    new TEdit (this, IDD_DeltaTime, MAX_NUMERIC);
    new TEdit (this, IDD_PointsToHide, MAX_NUMERIC);
    new TEdit (this, IDD_PointsToDraw, MAX_NUMERIC);

    AttractorGroup = new TGroupBox (this, IDD_AttractorGroup);
    new TRadioButton (this, IDD_JulianAttractor, AttractorGroup);
```

Enter the COMPLEXITY LAB

```
new TRadioButton (this, IDD_LorenzAttractor, AttractorGroup);
// ***** The following line is new code
new TRadioButton (this, IDD_CustomEquation, AttractorGroup);

SetTransferBuffer (tb);
}
```

Processing Your Own Equation

At this point you have provided a way for users to specify that they wish to use your equation. You now need to add the processing capability to actually respond appropriately to the user request. This is done in the WAttractorWindow class.

First, define a private Boolean variable that tells whether the custom equation radio button was selected. This is done in the private data area of the WAttractorWindow class header, as follows:

```
protected:
    // Protected data members ******************
    struct AttractorTransfer tb;
    struct TripleFloat Function; // function return values
    double CoefficientA; // attractor coefficients
    double CoefficientB;
    double CoefficientC;
    double XMin, XMax, YMin, YMax, ZMin, ZMax;

    double DeltaTime; // time step for numerical integration
    long PointsToHide; // hide initial points
    long PointsToDraw; // total points to draw
    BOOL JulianAttractor;
    BOOL LorenzAttractor;
    BOOL CustomAttractor;          // New code inserted here!!!!
```

In the WAttractorWindow source file, modify the initialization member function to initialize your new variable based on the transfer buffer.

```
void WAttractorWindow::InitializeVariables ()
{

    .
    .
    .

    JulianAttractor = tb.JulianAttractor;
    LorenzAttractor = tb.LorenzAttractor;
    CustomAttractor = tb.CustomAttractor;       // new code
```

Next, modify the CalculateNextPoint member function to calculate the next point to be plotted using your custom equation.

```
void WAttractorWindow::CalculateNextPoint ()
{

    struct TripleFloat EvaluatedFunction;


    // evaluate function at current location
    if (JulianAttractor == TRUE)
    {
        EvaluatedFunction.X = -Function.Y - Function.Z;
        EvaluatedFunction.Y = Function.X +
            (CoefficientA * Function.Y);
        EvaluatedFunction.Z =    CoefficientB +
                                    (Function.X * Function.Z) -
                                    (CoefficientC * Function.Z);
    }
    // **** begin of new inserted code
    else if (CustomAttractor == TRUE)
    {
        EvaluatedFunction.X = YOUR_CUSTOM_CODE;
        EvaluatedFunction.Y = YOUR_CUSTOM_CODE;
        EvaluatedFunction.Z = YOUR_CUSTOM_CODE;
    }
    // ***** end of new inserted code
    else
    {
        EvaluatedFunction.X =    (-CoefficientB * Function.X) +
                                    (Function.Z * Function.Y);
        EvaluatedFunction.Y =    (CoefficientC * Function.Z) -
                                    Function.Y -
                                    (Function.Z * Function.X);
        EvaluatedFunction.Z =    CoefficientA *
                                    (Function.Y - Function.Z);
    }

    // approximate next value using Euler's method (first order
method)
    Function.X += (DeltaTime * EvaluatedFunction.X);
    Function.Y += (DeltaTime * EvaluatedFunction.Y);
    Function.Z += (DeltaTime * EvaluatedFunction.Z);

}
```

If you want to add the capability to process a wide range of equations, you might want to change the preceding logic test from a series of `if...else` tests to a case statement. You might also consider replacing the radio buttons in the Setup dialog box with a combo box that contains a list of the available equations.

Enter the COMPLEXITY LAB

Tailoring the Fractals Lab

I've provided you with code that supports the Mandelbrot and Julia Set. You may want to experiment with graphic representations of equations other than these two sets. This can be easily accomplished using the approach described in this section.

Modifying the Setup Dialog Resource

You need to follow the procedures outlined for the Attractor Lab modifications to allow the user to specify the use of your custom equation. This is accomplished by adding the required define statement to the DCOMPLEX.H file, using the dialog editor in the Resource Workshop to add a new radio button for your equation, modifying the FractalTransfer transfer buffer in the WFRACTDI.H file to include an element for your new radio button, and modifying the WFractalDialog class by adding a line to create a radio button object corresponding to your new choice.

Processing Your Own Equation

To add processing for your own equation, modify the Update member function in the WFractalWindow class. This can be accomplished as follows:

```
void WFractalWindow::Update (RTMessage)
{
     RECT Rect;
     long double Real, Imaginary;
     long double DeltaX, DeltaY;
     long double ZReal, ZImaginary;
     long double CReal, CImaginary;
     long double TempLongDouble;
     int  Detail;

     Detail = atoi (tb.Detail);
     if (Detail < 16) Detail = 16; // minimum workable value

     GetClientRect (HWindow, &Rect);

     if (Row > Rect.bottom)
     {
         Stop ();
     }
     else
     {
         DeltaX = Right - Left;
         DeltaY = Bottom - Top;
         Imaginary = Top + (DeltaY * ((long double) Row /
Rect.bottom));
```

```
            HDC hDC = GetDC (HWindow);
            HDC hMemDC = CreateCompatibleDC (hDC);
            SelectObject (hMemDC, hBitmap);
            SetMapMode (hMemDC, GetMapMode (hDC));


            int Stop = Pixel + (int) (700 * CPUSpeed);
            for (; Pixel < Stop; Pixel++)
            {
                  if (Pixel >= Rect.right)
                  {
                        Pixel = 0;
                        Row++;
                        break;
                  }

                  Real = Left + (DeltaX * ((long double) Pixel /Rect.right));


                  if (tb.ChaoticCurl == TRUE)
                  {

                        CReal = -.74;
                        CImaginary = .11;
                        ZReal = Real;
                        ZImaginary = Imaginary;
                  }
//********** Begin custom inserted code *****************************
                  else if (tb.CustomEquation == TRUE)
                  {
                        CReal = YOUR_INITIAL_VALUE;
                        CImaginary = YOUR_INITIAL_VALUE;
                        ZReal = YOUR_INITIAL_VALUE;
                        ZImaginary = YOUR_INITIAL_VALUE;
                  }
// ************* End custom inserted code **************************

                  else // Julia set
                  {
                        CReal = Real;
                        CImaginary = Imaginary;
                        ZReal = 0.0;
                        ZImaginary = 0.0;
                  }


                  for (int Color = 1; Color < Detail; Color++)
                  {
//***************************************************************
```

Enter the COMPLEXITY LAB

```
// Add your test for divergence here. This can be made completely
different //from the Mandelbrot and Julia set by putting an if...else
test here using //the tb.CustomEquation variable for the test, or you
can use a variation on
// the Mandelbrot and Julia set by adding another divergence test to the
// existing if...else test embedded in this section of code.
//****************************************************************
                        // Square Z
                        TempLongDouble = ZReal * ZReal - ZImaginary * ZImaginary;
                        ZImaginary = ZReal * ZImaginary * 2;
                        ZReal = TempLongDouble;

                        // add the constant
                        ZReal += CReal;
                        ZImaginary += CImaginary;

                        if (sqrtl (ZReal * ZReal + ZImaginary * ZImaginary) > 2.0)
                        {
                              // convergence test
                              if (tb.Mandelbrot == TRUE)
                              {
                                    SetPixel (hDC, Pixel, Row, (COLORREF)
                                          (16777216l/Color));
                                    SetPixel (hMemDC, Pixel, Row,
                                          (COLORREF) (16777216l/Color));
                              }
                              else // tb.ChaoticCurl is true
                              {
                                    if (ZReal * ZReal + ZImaginary *
                                          ZImaginary> 4)
                                    {
                                          if (Color%2 == 0) // print for even
                                              {SetPixel (hDC, Pixel, Row,
                                                    (COLORREF) (16777216l/Color));
                                               SetPixel (hMemDC, Pixel, Row,
                                                    (COLORREF) (16777216l/Color));
                                          }
                                    }
                              }
                              break;
                        }
                  }
            }
      ReleaseDC (HWindow, hDC);
      DeleteDC (hMemDC);
      }
}
```

Tailoring the Boids Lab

I've hard-coded the rules that define the behavior of individual boids (and hence the emergent behavior exhibited by the flock). You may want to change this code to see how the flock behaves when individual boids behave differently. This can be easily accomplished using the approach described in this section.

Modifying an Individual Boid's Capabilities

Most of the individuality of a boid is embodied in its available data. The boids that I wrote store their current X and Y position, their desired velocity (expressed as a goal X and Y offset), and their color. If you want the Boids to store additional data you need to add the data elements to the WBoid header file and modify the ResetAll member function to initialize the data properly. Although you should make the data private, you do not generally need to provide access functions because the WBoid class declares that the WBoidWindow control class is a friend class, and it is therefore able to access WBoid private data.

Modifying the Control Program That Affects All Boids

The WBoidWindow class controls the behavior of the flock of Boids. The first step in adding your desired capability is to properly initialize the data variables to a starting value if the WBoid::ResetAll could not take care of it for you. This is accomplished in the WBoidWindow's ResetAll member function as follows:

```
void WBoidWindow::ResetAll ()
{
    RECT ClientArea;
    .
    .
    .

    // initialize the Boids
    for (i = 0; i < TotalBoids; i++)
    {
        BoidArray [i] = new WBoid();
        BoidArray [i]->SetPosition (random (ClientArea.right),
                         random (ClientArea.bottom));
        BoidArray [i]->GoalX = random (5) + 4;
        BoidArray [i]->GoalY = random (5) + 4;
        // Add your custom initialization here, if needed
    }
```

Enter the COMPLEXITY LAB

```
        // Clear the old rectangles from the screen
        InvalidateRect (HWindow, NULL, TRUE);
        UpdateWindow (HWindow);
}
```

The remaining task is to modify the Update member function to perform your custom processing. Each Boid's movement is controlled using a 10-by -10 matrix corresponding to possible new pixel locations. The Boid is currently at the center (4,4) of the matrix, so it can move as many as four pixels in either direction in the X and Y plane during each turn. The matrix values correspond to the attractiveness of a given new pixel location, with zero being neutral, positive being desirable, and negative being undesirable. The final position moved to will correspond to the highest cell value. In the event of a tie, a random cell from the winning entries is selected. I've annotated the Update member function code with the probable place where you will want to insert your new code.

```
void WBoidWindow::Update (RTMessage)
{
        RECT ClientRect;
        GetClientRect (HWindow, &ClientRect);
        int X, Y;
        int  Counter;


        HDC hDC = GetDC (HWindow);
        SetROP2 (hDC, R2_XORPEN);
        for (Counter = 0; Counter < (int) (10 * CPUSpeed); Counter++)
        {
            // Erase old boid
            BoidArray [Boid]->Draw (hDC);

            // now update positions
            InitChoices ();

            // Like to fly fast
            for (X =  2; X < 7; X++)
            {
                for (Y = 2; Y < 7; Y++)
                {
                    Choices[X][Y] -= TotalBoids / 3;
                }
            }
            // Don't sit still
            Choices [4][4] -= 100;

// ***** Here is where you probably will want to customize the code
```

```
                AvoidRectangles ();
                AvoidOtherBoids ();
                SeekCenterOfMass ();
                Choices [BoidArray[Boid]->GoalX][BoidArray[Boid]->GoalY] +=
                        TotalBoids / 4.5;

    // ***** End of where you probably will want to customize

                // Actually move the boid
                int MaxCell = -32000;
                int Total = 0;
                for (X = 0; X < 9; X++)
                {
                    for (Y = 0; Y < 9; Y++)
                    {
                        if (Choices[X][Y] > MaxCell)
                        {
                            MaxCell = Choices[X][Y];
                            Total = 0;
                        }
                        if (Choices[X][Y] == MaxCell) Total++;
                    }
                }

                // select from the candidate choices
                Total = random (Total);
                int NewX, NewY;
                if (Total == 0) Total = 1;
                while (Total > 0)
                {
                    for (X = 0; X < 9; X++)
                    {
                        for (Y = 0; Y < 9; Y++)
                        {
                            if (Choices[X][Y] == MaxCell)
                            {
                                Total—;
                                if (Total <= 0)
                                {
                                    NewX = X;
                                    NewY = Y;
                                    X = 10;
                                    break;
                                }
                            }
                        }
                    }
                }
                BoidArray[Boid]->CurrentX -= (4 - NewX);
                BoidArray[Boid]->CurrentY -= (4 - NewY);
```

Enter the COMPLEXITY LAB

```
    BoidArray[Boid]->GoalX = NewX;
    BoidArray[Boid]->GoalY = NewY;


    // handle the wrap-around at the edge of the world
    if (BoidArray[Boid]->CurrentX < 0)
        BoidArray[Boid]->CurrentX += ClientRect.right;
    if (BoidArray[Boid]->CurrentX > ClientRect.right)
        BoidArray[Boid]->CurrentX -= ClientRect.right;
    if (BoidArray[Boid]->CurrentY < 0)
        BoidArray[Boid]->CurrentY += ClientRect.bottom;
    if (BoidArray[Boid]->CurrentY > ClientRect.bottom)
        BoidArray[Boid]->CurrentY -= ClientRect.bottom;

    //Draw at new position
    BoidArray [Boid]->Draw (hDC);

    Boid++;
    if (Boid >= TotalBoids)
    {
        Boid = 0;
    }
    }
    ReleaseDC (HWindow, hDC);
}
```

Tailoring the Tapestry Lab

The most likely candidates for change in the Tapestry Lab are the initial
configuration of the cellular automaton or the rules that govern the transitions from one cycle to the next. You can easily control these factors using
the approach described in this section.

Changes in the Initial Configuration

The cellular automaton used by Tapestry is initialized in the member
function InitAutomaton. You can either modify one of the existing initialization routines or add a new capability by modifying the Setup dialog box to
include a radio button for your own initialization routine. The following
code fragment illustrates how this initialization is accomplished:

```
void WTapestryWindow::InitAutomaton ()
{
    RECT ClientRect;

    delete Automaton;
    Automaton = NULL;
```

```
// create automaton array
GetClientRect (HWindow, &ClientRect);
Automaton = new int [ClientRect.right];
memset (Automaton, 0, ClientRect.right * sizeof (int));

// initialize automaton array
int Colors = atoi (tb.Colors);
if (Colors > 255) Colors = 255;
if (Colors < 1) Colors = 1;
if (tb.Random == TRUE)
{
    time_t_T;

    srand((unsigned) time(&T));
    for (int i = 0; i < ClientRect.right; i++)
    {
        Automaton [i] = random (Colors);
    }
}
else if (tb.Repeated == TRUE)
{
    int Column = 0;
    int Index = 0;
    int Value = 0;
    Value = tb.Value [Index] - 'A';
    while (Column < ClientRect.right)
    {
        if (Value < 0) Value = 0;
        if (Value > Colors) Value = Colors;
        Automaton [Column++] = Value;
        Value = tb.Value [Index];
        if (Value == 0)
        {
            Index = 0;
            Value = tb.Value [Index] - 'A';
        }
        else
        {
            Value -= 'A';
            Index++;
        }
    }
}
else if (tb.Single == TRUE)
{
    int Value = 0;
    int Column = ClientRect.right / 2;
    Column -= strlen (tb.Value) / 2;
    if (Column < 0) Column = 0;
```

Enter the COMPLEXITY LAB

```
        for (int i = Column; i < Column + strlen (tb.Value); i++)
        {
            if (i >= ClientRect.right) break;
            Value = tb.Value [i - Column] - 'A';
            if (Value < 0) Value = 0;
            if (Value > Colors) Value = Colors;
            Automaton [i] = Value;
        }
    }
    // could add your own code here for another possibility
}
```

Changes in the Transition Rules

The Tapestry transition rules are specified in the InitRules member function. You can easily modify this routine to meet your own desires for initial
rules.

```
VOID WTapestryWindow::InitRules ()
{
    delete Rules;
    Rules = NULL;

    int Colors = atoi (tb.Colors);
    if (Colors > 255) Colors = 255;
    if (Colors < 1) Colors = 1;
    int Width = 5;
    if (tb.N3 == TRUE) Width = 3;
    else if (tb.N5 == TRUE) Width = 5;

    int TotalRules = Colors * Width;
    Rules = new int [TotalRules];

    memset (Rules, 0, TotalRules * sizeof (int));

    // initialize random number generator
    int RuleSeed = atoi (tb.RuleSeed);
    if (RuleSeed == 0)
    {
        time_t_T;
        srand((unsigned) time(&T));
    }
    else srand (RuleSeed);


    double Z = atof (tb.ZParam);
    if (Z > 1.0) Z = 1.0;
    if (Z < 0) Z = 0;
    int ZCheck = 0;
```

```
                    // Leave all black to all black, change rest
                    for (int i = 1; i < TotalRules; i++)
                    {
                        // determine if it should change based on Z
                        ZCheck = 100.0 * Z;
                        if (random (100) < ZCheck)
                        {
                            Rules [i] = random (Colors);
                        }
                    }
                }
```

This assumes that you are still using the basic definition of a transition rule as operating based on the sum of neighboring values for selecting a transition. For example, the Tapestry cellular automaton transition rules do not differentiate between 1-0-0 and 0-0-1 as cell values because they both total 1. If you choose to use a different strategy, you will need to modify both the InitRules member function and the Update member function, which is where the transition rules are actually applied.

Tailoring the Life Lab

You might want to experiment with the Life Lab by altering the rules that govern the cell transitions. This can be accomplished by modifying the Update member function in the WLife class.

```
void WLifeWindow::Update (RTMessage)
{
    int     i;

    for (i = 0; i < 10; i++)
    {

        for (int Col = 0; Col < 100; Col++)
        {

// The transition rules are hard coded into the section below

            if (Array [Col][ArrayRow] == TRUE)
            {
                if ((GetItemCount (ArrayRow, Col) != 2) &&
                    (GetItemCount (ArrayRow, Col) != 3))
                {
                    Array [Col][ArrayRow] = FALSE;
                }
            }
            else
            {
```

Enter the COMPLEXITY LAB

```
                    if (GetItemCount (ArrayRow, Col) == 3)
                    {
                            Array [Col][ArrayRow] = TRUE;
                    }
              }
// End of hard coded transition rules
          }

          PaintRow (ArrayRow);
          ArrayRow++;
          if (ArrayRow > 99)
          {
              ArrayRow = 0;
              InvalidateRect (HWindow, NULL, FALSE);
              UpdateWindow (HWindow);
          }
     }
}
```

Tailoring the Mice in a Maze Lab

The Mice in a Maze Lab has three main areas where you might want to
experiment: the rules used for sexual reproduction, the rules used for
mutation, and the way mice are selected for retention between generations.
This section addresses each of these areas.

Changing the Rules for Sexual Reproduction

The WMiceWindow class controls which mice should have sex with each other.
Actual sex between two mice is accomplished using the Sex member function of each mouse. This member function takes as an argument a pointer to
the WMice class that is the mate. As currently implemented, it is designed to
have each of the individual rules that govern behavior mate with the
corresponding rule in the other mouse. You might want to experiment with
sex that mates only some rules. The existing code looks like this:

```
void WMice::Sex (PWMice Mate)
{
     for (int i = 0; i < TotalRules; i++)
     {
          Rules[i]->Sex (Mate->Rules[i]);
     }
}
```

The WMouseRule class is responsible for knowing how to have sex with
another rule. The existing implementation breaks the rule apart into its
receptor, receptor mask (ReceptorDontCare), internal state, internal state

mask, output state, and effector and has each of these elements sexually merge with the corresponding element in the other rule. You may want to modify this to only have sex among certain portions of the rule, or to change the way you decide which portions should have sex with each other. Actual sex between portions of the rule is accomplished using a helper function called MergeRules. The existing code is as follows:

```
void WMouseRule::Sex (PWMouseRule Mate)
{
     MergeRules (Receptor, Mate->Receptor);
     MergeRules (ReceptorDontCare, Mate->ReceptorDontCare);
     MergeRules (State, Mate->State);
     MergeRules (StateDontCare, Mate->StateDontCare);
     MergeRules (StateOutput, Mate->StateOutput);
     MergeRules (Effector, Mate->Effector);
}
```

The MergeRules helper function randomly splices the two rule pieces together. The code makes use of the WBit class capabilities and works as follows:

```
void WMouseRule::MergeRules (RWBit Rule1, RWBit Rule2)
{
     for (int i = random ((int) Rule1.GetSize()); i < Rule1.GetSize();i++)
     {
          if (Rule2.Test(i) == 0) Rule1.Clear (i);
          else Rule1.Set (i);
     }
}
```

Changing the Rules for Mutation

Mutation is somewhat analogous with sex. The WMice class has a Mutate member function that is called by the WMouseWindow class. This member function takes a single parameter, the Rate, which is the mutation rate expressed as 1 mutation in Rate incidences. The WMouse's Mutate member function mutates each of its rules by calling the Mutate member function for that rule. The code is as follows:

```
void WMice::Mutate (int Rate)
{
     for (int i = 0; i < TotalRules; i++)
     {
          Rules[i]->Mutate (Rate);
     }
}
```

Enter the COMPLEXITY LAB

The MouseRule's Mutate member function individually mutates each part of the rule (the receptor, receptor mask, internal state, internal state mask, output state, and effector). You might want to mutate only part of the WMouseRule's internal components. This mutation is accomplished using the WMouseRule's MutateBits helper function. The Mutate code is as follows:

```
void WMouseRule::Mutate (int Odds)
{
    // mutates one out of every Odds bits

    MutateBits (ReceptorDontCare, Odds);
    MutateBits (Receptor, Odds);
    MutateBits (StateDontCare, Odds);
    MutateBits (State, Odds);
    MutateBits (StateOutput, Odds);
    MutateBits (Effector, Odds);
}
```

The MutateBits helper function simply takes the bit array and randomly toggles the bits with the proper probability. Some algorithmic changes might improve the efficiency of this routine and still result in sufficient randomness in the mutations to meet your requirements.

```
void WMouseRule::MutateBits (RWBit Bits, int Odds)
{

    long BitSize = Bits.GetSize ();

    for (long i = 0; i < BitSize; i++)
    {
        if (random (Odds) == 0)
        {
            Bits.Toggle (i);
        }
    }

}
```

Changing the Way Mice Are Selected for the Next Generation

When it is time for a new generation of mice, the WMouseWindow's NewGeneration member function is called. As currently written, this routine reorders the mice in accordance with their success in achieving the objectives (using the ReorderMouseArray member function), then reproduces the successful mice using the MouseReproduce member function. The code is as follows:

```
void WMiceWindow::NewGeneration ()
{

    RECT ClientRect;

    ReorderMouseArray ();
    MouseReproduce ();
    if (tb.MiceSex == TRUE) MouseSex ();
    MouseMutate ();
    InitRectangles ();
    InitCheese ();

    GetClientRect (HWindow, &ClientRect);
    for (int i = 0; i < TotalMice; i++)
    {
        MiceArray [i]->SetPosition (10, ClientRect.bottom - 10);
    }
    InvalidateRect (HWindow, NULL, TRUE);
    UpdateWindow (HWindow);
}
```

The `ReorderMouseArray` member function sorts the mice by their proximity to the cheese. As written, I use an approximation of the distance based on summing the X and Y distances (as opposed to the actual distance, which is the square root of the sum of the X and Y squared). I also make a major simplification by not considering the fact that the shortest path to the cheese may involve exiting the world and reentering on the other side (recall that the maze is a toroid). For example, if the cheese is in the bottom-right corner of the maze and the mouse is in the upper-left corner, the mouse is actually very close, assuming that it moves northwest in direction. This simplification does not come into play when the cheese is kept at the center of the maze (the default condition). You may wish to change the criteria used for performing the sort. Some faster sorting algorithms can also be used if you want to improve the performance of this code. The existing code is as follows:

```
void WMiceWindow::ReorderMouseArray ()
{
    // Reorder in descending order based on approx. distance
    // from the cheese
    int i, j;
    PWMice Temp;
    int Index;
    int  Smallest;
    POINT P;
    int *Distance = new int [TotalMice];
```

Enter the COMPLEXITY LAB

```
for (i = 0; i < TotalMice; i++)
{
    P.x = MiceArray [i]->CurrentX;
    P.y = MiceArray [i]->CurrentY;
    Distance [i] = abs (P.x - Cheese.x);
    Distance [i] += abs (P.y - Cheese.y);
}

for (i = 0; i < TotalMice; i++)
{
    // Put the next closest Mouse in this slot
    // first, find the smallest element
    Smallest = 32000;
    Index = 0;
    for (j = i; j < TotalMice; j++)
    {
        if (Distance [j] < Smallest)
        {
            Smallest = Distance [j];
            Index = j;
        }
    }

    // Now swap the Mice Array Entries
    Temp = MiceArray [i];
    MiceArray [i] = MiceArray [Index];
    MiceArray [Index] = Temp;

    // Now swap the Distance Array Entries
    int TempInt;
    TempInt = Distance [i];
    Distance[i] = Distance [Index];
    Distance [Index] = TempInt;
}
delete [] Distance;
}
```

The actual reproduction of the successful mice is accomplished in the
MouseReproduce member function. As written, it simply takes the top 10
percent of the mice and randomly copies them into the bottom 90 percent
that have now died. You might want to change the percent that you keep
alive (or make this a user choice). You could also build more intelligence
into this routine by having it recognize the mice that have successfully
arrived at the cheese and keep all of these mice (or alternately modify the
ReorderMouseArray to put mice earlier in the array that got to the cheese

faster). Another possible change is to use a lottery-type approach for deciding who lives and who dies, with more successful mice having a higher probability of living but less successful mice having at least a shot at life. The existing code is as follows:

```
void WMiceWindow::MouseReproduce ()
{
    int  Keep = TotalMice / 10;
    for (int i = Keep; i < TotalMice; i++)
    {
        *MiceArray[i] = MiceArray [random (Keep)];
    }
}
```

Enter the COMPLEXITY LAB

Appendix

B

Shareware

SOFTWARE

*More Complexity
programs, available
as shareware for you to
explore and investigate*

High-quality shareware that allows you to further explore various aspects of complexity software is available on various bulletin boards. I've included three such programs with this book. Please feel free to experiment with the software. If you find it useful and want to continue to experiment with it, I encourage you to support the shareware concept by sending the program's authors the requested fees (which are quite nominal). The three programs I am including are

- Mandelbrot—A sophisticated program that enables you to view the Mandelbrot set from a variety of perspectives.
- Life—An advanced version of the game of life. The most valuable aspect of this shareware version is a set of files containing initial configurations for a wide variety of patterns that demonstrate interesting behavior.
- Galaxy—A program that models gravitational attraction between stars and demonstrates emergent behavior on a galactic scale.

Mandelbrot Shareware Program

Figure B.1 shows the initial screen of the Mandelbrot program after being maximized. Selecting Effects from the main menu displays the dialog box shown in Figure B.2. You can select Edge Tracing to draw a form of contour lines with equal tendency to diverge, as shown in Figure B.3.

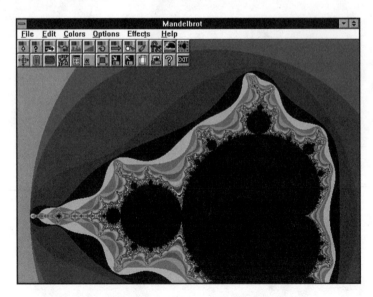

Figure B.1.
The initial screen of the Mandelbrot program, after it has been maximized.

Enter the COMPLEXITY LAB

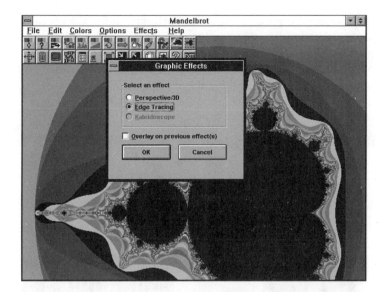

Figure B.2.
The Effects dialog box.

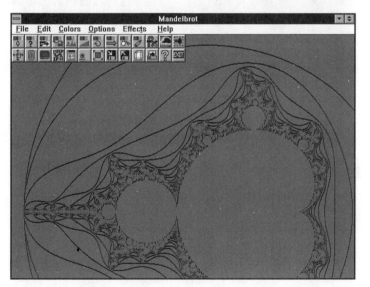

Figure B.3.
Edge Tracing of the Mandelbrot set.

You can also select the Perspective radio button from the Effects dialog box. The Perspective dialog box (Figure B.4) enables you to specify the three-dimensional perspective you are interested in along with a number of special effects. Figure B.5 shows a three-dimensional perspective, with height (stand-up at 15 percent) added to the countours.

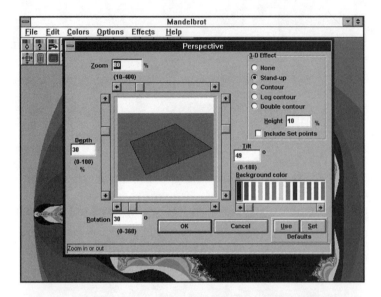

Figure B.4.
The Perspective dialog box.

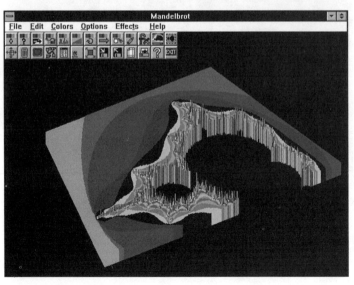

Figure B.5.
A three-dimensional perspective with height.

Enter the COMPLEXITY LAB

The Colors menu gives you a wide variety of control over the colors used to draw the Mandelbrot Set. The Animate option is particularly fascinating, as it animates the color palette and makes the set seem to grow and shrink dynamically. Figure B.6 shows the set with an alternate color scheme following a zoom.

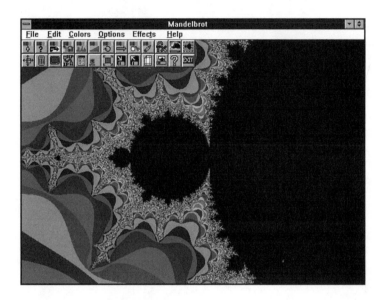

Figure B.6.
Zoomed Mandelbrot set with alternate color scheme.

Life Shareware Program

Figure B.7 shows the initial screen of the Life program following maximization. You begin by selecting Edit, then Random Cells, from the main menu to initialize the matrix. You also can select File, then Open, to load a specific initial configuration that demonstrates a particularly interesting cell arrangement. Select Run, then Grow, from the main menu to start Life working. The Options allow you to control the colors of the cells and the background. Figure B.8 shows the game working after starting with a random configuration. Figure B.9 shows the results using FACTORY.LIF as a starting point. The cells continue to reproduce gliders that are dispatched to the outside world. A wide variety of other interesting initial configurations are included as .LIF files, although most are more interesting as animated patterns to observe on the computer rather than static patterns to see in a picture.

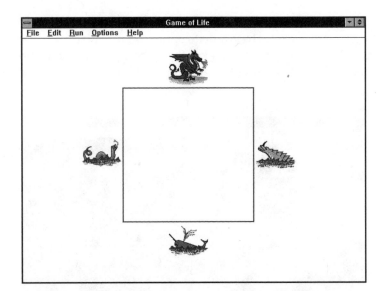

Figure B.7.
The initial screen of Life.

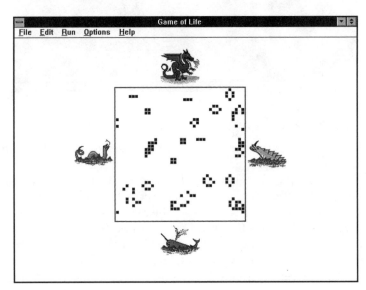

Figure B.8.
Life beginning with a random configuration.

Enter the COMPLEXITY LAB

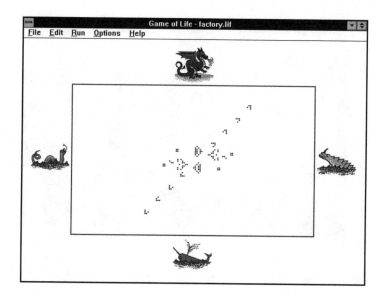

Figure B.9.
Life starting with the FACTORY.LIF file.

Galaxy Shareware Program

Figure B.10 shows the Setup dialog box for Galaxy. I use this to specify the desired number of stars, but I leave the other parameters alone. To actually draw the stars on the screen, select Init from the main menu. Figure B.11 shows the initial screen with 200 stars displayed. You can animate the screen by selecting Run from the main menu, and then watch emergent behavior on a galactic scale. We would expect to see emergent behavior in this system because the individual components all interact. I would expect that the behavior of individual simulated stars would vary between chaotic and stable. The stability would be observed in outlying stars that are minimally influenced by the other stars and by stars that are in the center and locked into predictable patterns. The remaining stars would be chaotic as they move between various regions of stability in a difficult-to-predict fashion. Selecting Run again stops the animation. Selecting Exit exits the program. On my computer, I noticed that if I exited the program by double-clicking the upper-left corner of the window, it locked up my computer and forced me to reset. I did not have any similar problems when exiting using the Cancel menu choice.

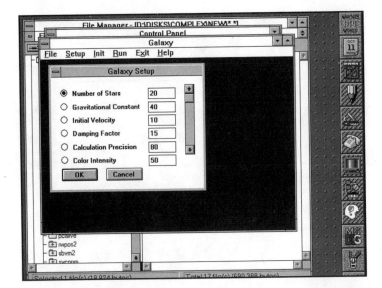

Figure B.10.
The Galaxy Setup dialog box.

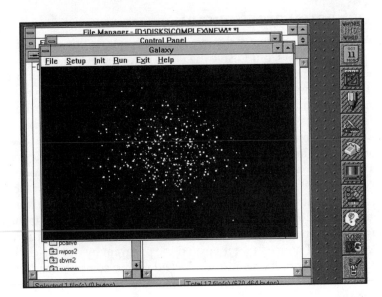

Figure B.11.
The Galaxy initial screen, 200 stars.

Enter the COMPLEXITY LAB

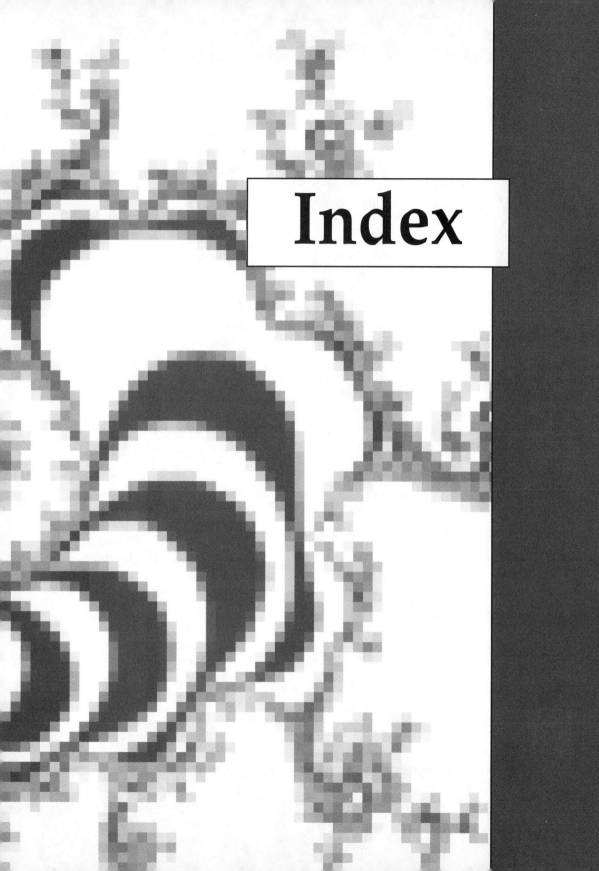

Index

Enter the COMPLEXITY LAB

Enter the COMPLEXITY LAB

Enter the COMPLEXITY LAB

Enter the COMPLEXITY LAB

Enter the COMPLEXITY LAB

Enter the COMPLEXITY LAB

Add to Your Sams Library Today with the Best Books for Programming, Operating Systems, and New Technologies

The easiest way to order is to pick up the phone and call

1-800-428-5331

between 9:00 a.m. and 5:00 p.m. EST.
For faster service please have your credit card available.

ISBN	Quantity	Description of Item	Unit Cost	Total Cost
0-672-30373-6		On the Cutting Edge of Technology	$22.95	
0-672-30299-3		Uncharted Windows Programming (Book/Disk)	$34.95	
0-672-30301-9		Artificial Life Explorer's Kit (Book/Disk)	$24.95	
0-672-30361-2		Virtual Reality and the Exploration of Cyberspace (Book/Disk)	$26.95	
0-672-30270-5		Garage Virtual Reality (Book/Disk)	$29.95	
0-672-30320-5		Morphing Magic	$29.95	
0-672-30315-9		The Magic of Image Processing (Book/Disk)	$39.95	
0-672-30308-6		Tricks of the Graphics Gurus (Book/Disk)	$49.95	
0-672-30362-0		Navigating the Internet	$24.95	
0-672-30413-9		Multimedia Madness!, Deluxe Ed. (Book/CD-ROM)	$49.95	
0-672-30322-1		PC Video Madness! (Book/CD-ROM)	$39.95	
0-672-30352-3		Blaster Mastery (Book/Disk/CD-ROM)	$34.95	
0-672-30347-7		Fractal Graphics for Windows (Book/Disk/CD)	$39.95	
0-672-30274-8		Mastering Borland C++, 2E (Book/Disk)	$39.95	
0-672-30137-7		Secrets of Borland C++ Masters (Book/Disk)	$44.95	
0-672-30060-5		Developing Windows Applications with Borland C++ 3.1, 2E	$39.95	
☐ 3 ½" Disk		Shipping and Handling: See information below.		
☐ 5 ¼" Disk		TOTAL		

Shipping and Handling: $4.00 for the first book, and $1.75 for each additional book. Floppy disk: add $1.75 for shipping and handling. If you need to have it NOW, we can ship product to you in 24 hours for an additional charge of approximately $18.00, and you will receive your item overnight or in two days. Overseas shipping and handling adds $2.00 per book and $8.00 for up to three disks. Prices subject to change. Call for availability and pricing information on latest editions.

201 W. 103rd Street, Indianapolis, Indiana 46290

1-800-428-5331 — Orders   1-800-835-3202 — FAX   1-800-858-7674 — Customer Service

Book ISBN 0-672-30395-7

What's on the Disk

Labs on the disk allow you to venture into the world of complexity by manipulating various aspects of this fascinating science.

Lab	Aspect of Complexity
■ Attractor	Stability and Chaos
■ Fractal	Chaos
■ Boids	Emergent Behavior
■ Tapestry	One-Dimensional Cellular Automata
■ Life	Multi-Dimensional Cellular Automata
■ Mice in a Maze	Genetic Algorithms

Plus, you'll find these shareware complexity/chaos programs:

- ■ Mandelbrot
- ■ The Game of Life
- ■ Galaxy

Note: You need Microsoft™ Windows 3.1, a 386 or 486 computer, 4M of memory, a mouse, and VGA-compatible graphics to run these programs.

Installing the Floppy disk

The software included with this book is stored in a compressed format. You must run the installation program on the floppy disk to install the software. You'll need at least 2M of free space on your hard drive.

1. From Windows File Manager, or Program Manager, choose **F**ile | **R**un from the menu.

2. Type `<drive>`INSTALL and press Enter. `<drive>` is the letter of the drive that contains the installation disk. For example, if the disk is in drive B:, type `B:INSTALL` and press Enter.

Follow the on-screen instructions in the install program. The files will be installed to a directory named \COMPLEX, unless you change this during the installation program.

A Program Manager group named "Enter the Complexity Lab" will be created by the installation program. Appendix B contains information on the bonus shareware programs.